Handmade Furniture

21 Classic Woodworking Projects to Build for Your Home

By Rafael Nathan

Linden Publishing
Fresno, California

Handmade Furniture: 21 Classic Woodworking Projects to Build for Your Home
© Rafael Nathan

First published in 2011 by Interwood Holdings Pty Ltd, Australia. First Linden edition 2014.

Author: Rafael Nathan
Editor : Linda Nathan
Designer: Gabriela Dias

Photo credits: All photos by author except as noted—Cover photo (also on p.81) by Jon Linkin. Images on pp.6, 9, 12, 16, 22, 32, 42, 46, 51, 55, 62, 66, 67, 72, 92, 98 by Rebecca Nathan. Images on pp. 36, 83, 84, 105, 108 by Roger Phillips.

Linden Publishing titles may be purchased in quantity at special discounts for educational, business, or promotional use. To inquire about discount pricing, please refer to the contact information below. For permission to use any portion of this book for academic purposes, please contact the Copyright Clearance Center at www.copyright.com.

Woodworking is inherently dangerous. Your safety is your responsibility. Neither Linden Publishing nor the author assume any responsibility for any injuries or accidents.

All the pieces in this book were made using metric measurements. In converting these to imperial some rounding-off was used. To avoid any problems please allow for these conversions when making your own pieces with imperial measurements.

ISBN: 978-1-61035-210-9
Printed in China
135798642

Library of Congress Cataloging-in-Publication Data
Nathan, Rafael, 1952-
   Handmade furniture : 21 classic woodworking projects to build for your home / by Rafael Nathan.
      pages cm
   ISBN 978-1-61035-210-9 (paperback)
1. Furniture making. I. Title.
TT194.N38 2014
684.1--dc23

                                    2013043240

Linden Publishing, Inc.
2006 S. Mary, Fresno, CA 93721
www.lindenpub.com / 1-800-345-4447

Foreword

The projects presented here first appeared in *Australian Wood Review* magazine, although the format here is different and some revisions and additions have been made.

These projects are grouped by kind as trays, boxes, and cabinets and tables, so the level of difficulty varies. If you are just starting to do woodwork you might first tackle the End Grain Breadboard and Sushi Trays, followed by the Toolbox and Blackwood Hall Table.

Making things is important to me, often more so than the objects themselves. I'm self-taught, and after 30 years I'm still learning. Hand skills are critical, even for those who use power tools and machinery. When I started learning how to work wood I spent most nights at home after work teaching myself basic wood skills like sawing and planing. I would make rows of knife cuts across a board and hand saw and plane these till there was no wood left. I made simple shelves and planter boxes and sold them at weekend markets. I got a job at a furniture factory, got sacked, got re-hired, managed the place, then started my own workshop in a tiny room at home. I made kitchens, batches of recycled wood furniture, opened a shop, sold a shop, and moved to a bush block. It's a rare day when I don't spend time in the shop.

Learning what does and doesn't work visually and structurally is part of the journey. The projects in this book are part of my own trip, so to speak. You can use the plans and techniques to make these and other designs that suit your tastes, needs and the wood you have at hand.

The choice of timbers reflects my own preferences. I like to combine species that seem to balance each other color-wise, or use the grain of some species in ways that seem to complement them. Feel free to substitute your own choices of woods available in your area.

All of the pieces in this book were made using metric measurements. In converting these to imperial some rounding-off was used. To avoid any problems please allow for these conversions when making your own pieces with imperial measurements.

Safety needs to be paramount in your mind when you work wood. Hand and power tools, and machines with high-speed cutters need to be used with mindful concentration. Make sure you plan your work and organize your workspace and workflow so you can apply full attention to the task at hand.

The projects presented here are yours to experiment with. I wish you success with your woodworking.

—Raf Nathan

contents

Storage and Boxes

Cabinets

Made using simple

techniques, this attractive

breadboard makes

an excellent gift.

End Grain Breadboard

E veryone needs a breadboard cum cutting board and while it is true that any piece of wood will do the job nothing beats a nicely made object that has had care put into its making.

This is a good project for beginners—you can practise cutting, dressing and gluing up wood in a way that's not going to cost you too much if things go wrong.

I've made a traditional end grain style of cutting board, also called a butchers block. The end grain wears well under constant cutting use.

I am using square dressed blackwood but you can choose other species, ideally 'neutral' woods like pine or ash. Celery top and kauri pine are also suitable for this purpose because they are 'tasteless' and odourless.

Basically the process is to glue up blocks of wood into a panel, plane this flat, slice sections off and then reglue the sections.

FIRST GLUE-UP

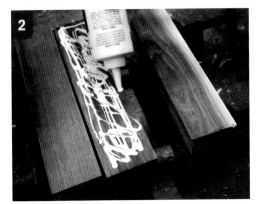

The wood I used started at 2³/₄ x 2³/₄" (70 x 70mm). Before any gluing takes place the wood needs to be planed down to 2³/₄ x 2¹/₂" (70 x 65mm). Glue the wood together with the 2³/₄" (70mm) thickness vertical (looking from above, the pieces are 2¹/₂" (65mm) wide).

Use a non-toxic water-resistant or waterproof PVA based glue such as Titebond. There are other glues like polyurethane which may be waterproof but find out if they are toxic. Apply glue liberally and use plenty of clamps.

Leave the glue-up to dry overnight and then plane the panel flat on both sides. I ran the panel through my thicknesser for this. This is why the original pieces were planed to 2¹/₂" (65mm) wide. You now plane the panel down to 2¹/₂" thick making all the individual end grain pieces 2¹/₂" square.

SECOND GLUE-UP

Using the tablesaw I sliced off 1³/₈" (35mm) wide sections of wood, which seemed to me a good thickness for a breadboard. I used the fence as a length stop for this.

To avoid problems with wood movement I had already set up a glue area so that as soon as the wood was sliced it was glued. I did not want components lying around and risk any twisting or cupping.

The square alignment of the wood should be near perfect. Apply glue and rub two pieces together until they 'grab', then add another strip. Also keep everything flush as possible on the top.

Once again use plenty of clamps.

When dry, the excess glue can be chiselled off.

DETAILS AND SANDING

The edges will need to be planed smooth and flat.

Low angle planes like the one being used here were apparently developed for butcher block work like this. These planes handle end grain very well.

After flattening with the plane I used the belt sander to really get things moving. I started with 60 grit and worked my way through 80 and 100 grit then changed to a random orbit sander for progressively finer sanding.

The edges were detailed by running a block plane at around 45°.

APPLY A FINISH

I applied numerous coats of olive oil over a couple of days. You could add a handle so the board can be hung up if you wish. Please note a wood product like this should never be immersed in water or placed in the dishwasher.

Sushi Trays

When making small items to either give or sell it's good to keep costs down. This project fits a number of criteria that will help do this. The material cost is minimal—shorts of most woods are readily available. Machining and sanding requirements are straightforward and simple, and hopefully the end product is desirable.

These sushi trays are made from Douglas fir. Breadboard ends like these are a stretch on allowing for wood movement. However the panels are only 5½" (140mm) wide and well dried quartersawn timber is always preferred. Use a PVA adhesive which has some flexibility.

For three trays there are three panels and six breadboard ends. The panels are 11" (280mm) long, 5½" (140mm) wide and ³/₈" (10mm) thick. The breadboard ends are 5½" long, 1-³/₄" (45mm) wide and ³/₄" thick.

Lay the pieces together and mark out where the joints will be. Dowels, biscuits or dominos can be used. The joints can be now cut.

Sand the underneath of the panels before assembly.

Apply glue then work quickly to bring the panels and ends together.

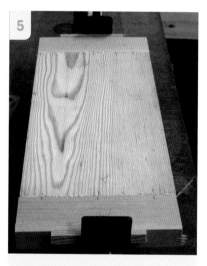

Clamp the assembly together.

Check everything is flat and true with a straightedge. Leave to dry overnight.

After the glue is dry any squeeze-out can be removed with a chisel.

Mark a line where the finger cut-out will be. Note how the third finger is pressing against the wood and this acts as a stop for the pencil. Running the pencil along like this gives an accurate line to work to. You don't always need to use a marking gauge or tape measure to mark a guide line.

The first pass on the router table removes part of the finger cut-out. Remove a little more on the second pass. The piece of wood under the tray gives support.

A third pass on the router table removes the last of the waste for the cut-out.

A block plane can soften the inside edge and mirror the cut-out. The piece of scrap under the block plane protects the tray surface from marking.

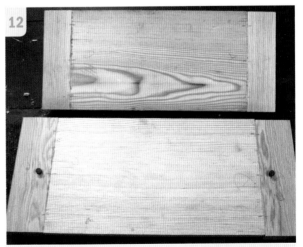

The trays are now complete but I drilled a small hole and glued in a contrasting dowel to add a detail. At this point the trays can be fine sanded and prepared for polishing. In this case they were polished with a spray lacquer. Alternatives are a water based varnish or shellac.

Dovetail Gifts

Here are two small gift ideas

that will get you dovetailing.

The dovetail is one of those things that people readily identify with quality woodwork. However it can also be quite a difficult joint to execute. Do it badly and people will notice immediately and all your other good work will pale into the background.

The tray and box shown above should help you establish some dovetail skills, they certainly helped mine. There are a couple of ways to cheat with the making of dovetails, either use a dedicated jig with a router, or a handsaw guide. A router jig will do the whole thing while a handsaw guide still requires you to mark out correctly and chisel away waste. I don't have a router jig but have used them in the past and they do work well.

Here I'm using a Veritas guide and it does a good job of guiding the saw during a cut providing the dovetail is no longer than 1" (25mm) or so—like any tool the more you use it the better the results. In the box project the jig can be used for sawing both tails and pins. With the tray, the tail is $1^3/_4$" (45mm) long so there was some slight deviance using the jig but it still sawed better than I would do freehand. The pin part of the dovetail

on the end pieces for the tray were too wide for the jig to be used so this was done freehand. If your sawing skills are not up to par you can saw close to the line and then use a chisel to pare down to the line.

My own style for freehand sawing is to try and use gravity. Have the wood being sawn held firmly in a vice or clamped to the bench as close to plumb (true vertical) as possible. Try and have a relaxed posture and let gravity guide the saw down, the rest is practice. I use a knife line to work to—this makes the process both easier and harder. It's harder to work to a knife line, but ultimately it's easier, because as long as you respect the line, everything is guaranteed to go together snugly.

These projects use contrasting wood to highlight the dovetail. The box uses Huon pine and silky oak while the tray uses Huon pine and blackwood. I suggest making a box or two first and then try the tray. Normally you would not glue a piece of wood across as I have done on the tray panel as it would restrict timber movement. I have broken the rules here for the sake of the look I was after.

Making the tray

1. The tails are sawn first on the Huon pine and then a line is scribed with a cutting gauge to define the shoulders.

2. With the tails sawn and shoulders chiselled the lighter wood is held in place over the end pieces. The dimensions of the tails is random depending on what you think looks the best.

3. Saw and chisel are used to remove the waste. A router or laminate trimmer can also be utilised to remove the waste up to the line. This will give you a good accurate flat area.

4. Finished tail opening.

5. A batten and clamps bring the tray panel and ends together.

CUTTING LIST		Measurements in inches/mm		
QTY	COMPONENT	LENGTH	WIDTH	THICKNESS
1	panel	15 (380)	7½ (190)	³⁄₈ (10)
2	ends	7½ (190)	1³⁄₄ (45)	1 (25)

The cut on the right is too close to the knife line. The left cut is much better as it leaves the line intact.

CUTTING LIST
Measurements in inches/mm

QTY	COMPONENT	LENGTH	WIDTH	THICKNESS
2	sides	$12^{1}/_{4}$ (310)	$1^{1}/_{2}$ (40)	$^{3}/_{8}$ (9)
2	ends	$3^{1}/_{4}$ (80)	$1^{1}/_{2}$ (40)	$^{3}/_{4}$ (20)
1	base	$12^{1}/_{4}$ (310)	$3^{1}/_{4}$ (80)	$^{3}/_{16}$ (4)
1	divider	$2^{1}/_{2}$ (62)	3 (76)	$^{3}/_{8}$ (9)

Making the box

1. All the wood components are first planed and sawn to size. Two sides can be marked and sawn at once.

2. I used a saw guide to make the cuts. The silky oak was reasonably easy to work. Harder timbers are naturally more difficult to saw. Of course you don't have to use a saw guide, freehand is always better.

3. The two saw cuts have been made and the shoulders now need to be sawn. I marked the depth of cut with a pencil. After sawing I marked the shoulders with a cutting gauge. The whole thing is about working to a knife mark, not a pencil line. I used the pencil initially and then the cutting gauge because I didn't want a knife mark showing.

4. I'm using a Veritas straight guide to make the shoulder cuts. The saw is set to cut on the right of the cutting gauge mark. While the finish off the saw may be good it often still requires some cleaning up with a chisel and of course needs to be checked for square.

5. The tail now needs to be held against the box end and the pins marked. A small Japanese brass clamp is great for clamping small things. I find it best to mark the pins with a knife.

6. The Veritas saw guide can be used to make the pin cuts. After this, drill out some of the waste and remove the rest with a chisel.

7. Once the joints are made and checked the box can be glued up. Sand the inside faces before glue up and check that all is square. The base is $^{3}/_{16}$" (4mm) thick solid timber and can be glued on afterwards as can the center divider.

8. A reasonably good result. The outside can be planed and sanded when all the gluing is completed. Choice of finish is open, oil and wax are probably the easiest to apply.

A Table with Flare

Shaped legs and low key details characterise this Huon pine hall table.

The main feature of this table is the curved legs. The leg design originates from a project by John Makepeace in a book titled *The Woodwork Book* (Pan Books). John Makepeace was one of my favourite wood heroes in the 1970s. His work was quite radical in design but retained traditional woodwork values in construction. His furniture making school at Parnham achieved legendary status but unfortunately no longer operates.

The original table Makepeace designed was from English elm, and used much thicker timber sections for the drawer rails and top. I decided to use Huon pine. Makepeace gives specific measurements for the leg shape. The two inside faces of the leg are straight,

while the base flares out to 2³/₄" (70mm) and the top of the leg is 2" (50mm) square. Around one third of the way down from the top the leg is 1¹/₂" (40mm) square. These are your fixed measurements and a gentle curve then needs to be traced connecting these points up. To make this curve I flexed a steel rule between the points and then marked the curve with a pencil. It is critical, however, to make a plywood or MDF template of this leg shape, which should be your first step.

The front drawer rails are ³/₄" (20mm) thick. The top rail is 2" wide to match the size of the leg at the top and the lower rail around 1¹/₂" (40–42mm) wide. For ease of manufacture I machined both rails to 2" and sawed the lower rail down to size later. The table sides and rear rails, also ³/₄" thick, are 5¹/₄" (136mm) wide. The vertical drawer divider is 2" wide and decorated with two inlaid blackwood strips. When preparing the vertical divider I allowed quite a bit of extra length which provided the decorative insert for the backpiece on the tabletop. This backpiece is 1" (25mm) high and adds a design detail to the top.

Getting started

Prepare the legs for the table—these are 2³/₄"x 2³/₄" (70 x 70mm) square, and 29¹/₂" (750mm) long. Trace the curve onto the leg blank and carefully bandsaw away the waste. Where possible, try and have the grain of the wood following the sweep of the leg curve. For a consistent shape on all the legs I used a template-following router cutter **(photo 1).** This cutter has a ballbearing mounted near the collet which rides along the plywood template **(photo 2).** After one full pass with the router **(photo 3),** the next pass dispenses with the template and the bearing follows the finished surface of the wood. By carefully controlling the router and not removing too much timber in one pass, a very clean surface can be obtained direct from the power tool. Final sanding, which can be done before assembly, is all that is required to achieve a smooth finish on the curve.

The two front rail joints can now be prepared. The top rail connects to the leg with a lapped dovetail, which is reasonably easy to cut. The lower rail uses two stub tenons—in this instance two tenons are better than one larger one, which would remove too much timber from the leg and weaken the structure **(photo 4).**

The template mounted on a leg and the router used to shape the leg.

First pass with the router yields a stepped cut. The next pass without the template completes the leg.

The side rails use one large tenon each, and the rear rail has two smaller tenons. Take care in laying these out so that there is sufficient clearance for each mortise and tenon **(photo 5).** I used a slot mortising machine to cut the mortises in the legs and cleaned up the corners with a chisel. I first marked the tenons with the marking gauge **(photo 6).** The tenons were cut using a router **(photo 7).** By using a fence, which the router rides against, a square shoulder can be cut in the timber. Have an offcut available to check tenon sizes before working the actual tenons on the rails. Tenons were sized with a vernier gauge **(photo 8).**

As mentioned, the vertical drawer divider has blackwood inlay. A piece of wood was passed over the tablesaw with the blade protruding $1/8$" (2mm) to make a shallow trench. Blackwood strips were planed to size and glued into the trenches. When dry, the blackwood was planed level with the surface. The divider can be joined to the horizontal rails by using short stub tenons, or as I have seen on some excellent antiques, countersunk screws can be used to hold it in place.

The internal drawer runners need to be prepared and joints cut. Biscuits are an excellent choice for these. The side drawer runners can have a biscuit at the front and rear to locate them in the rails. The drawer guides can be simply screwed and glued in place.

Front leg joints. Lapped dovetail at top and twin stub tenons. The side rail has a large tenon. The lower rail yet to be sawn down to meet the leg curve.

Rear leg joints. Note how the tenons clear each other.

The tenons marked.

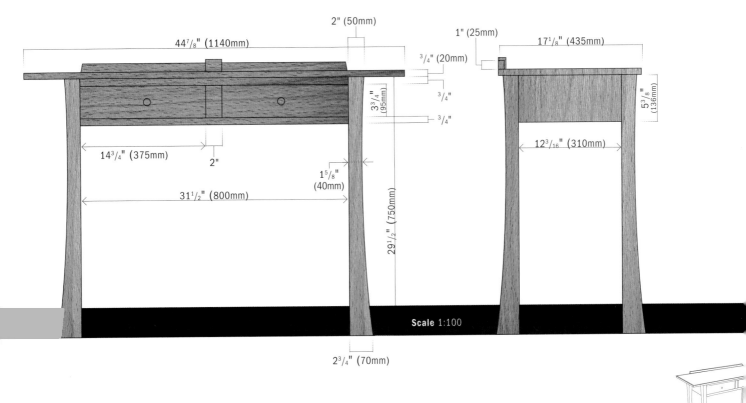

2" (50mm)

44⁷/₈" (1140mm)

1" (25mm)

17¹/₈" (435mm)

³/₄" (20mm)

³/₄"

3³/₄" (95mm)

5³/₈" (136mm)

³/₄"

14³/₄" (375mm)

2"

1⁵/₈" (40mm)

31¹/₂" (800mm)

12³/₁₆" (310mm)

29¹/₂" (750mm)

Scale 1:100

2³/₄" (70mm)

A TABLE WITH FLARE

Base assembly

With all components machined and jointed, do a test assembly before gluing up. Glue the front legs and rails together first, including the vertical drawer divider. It is critical that this section is square and has no twist. The rear legs and rear rail can also be assembled, once again checking for square. Leave these to dry overnight. The next day the side rails can be glued in place to complete the table structure. At this stage, the drawer runners should also be glued in place.

Now is a good time to glue up the tabletop and place this aside to dry. I used ³/₄" (20mm) thick timber for this, however in retrospect I think 1¹/₄" (32mm) would have better complemented the fullness in the base of the legs. While the top is top drying, additional work can be done to the drawer runners, such as fitting the drawer guides.

Drawers

The drawers were made with Huon pine fronts, sides and backs. Measurements from these were taken directly from the table openings. The best joints to use for the drawer fronts and sides are dovetails. The sides and backs can be joined with small ¹/₄" (6mm) dowels **(photos 9 and 10)**. I used a dowelling jig for the backs and a drill press for the sides. I sawed grooves in the fronts and sides to accept plywood bases.

Routing the tenons.

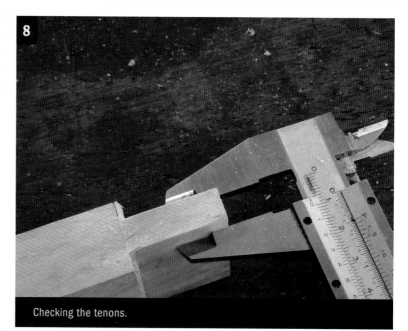

Checking the tenons.

Drawer knobs

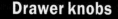

You can choose from a selection of ready-made drawer knobs according to your preference. I purchased brass insert knobs from an American company, Bridge City Tools. These require a wooden plug to be cut and glued in place. Once the glue is dry the plug can be sanded level with the brass. These insert knobs are reasonably expensive but add a distinctive and refined touch to the finished piece.

Because of the tapered curve in the leg, the lower section of the drawer front will need to planed down. Fit the drawer into the opening and mark how much timber is to be removed, taking care to leave a reasonable amount of wood in the front so as not to weaken the lower dovetail. You will then need to plane the drawer face down to your line, constantly checking that the curve matches the line of the table leg.

Fitting the top

The top will need to be planed and sanded flat, and then sized. A small 45° bevel is routed on its upper edge. The top is secured to the table frame by the use of wooden buttons. The buttons match slots in the rails cut with a biscuit jointer.

The backpiece on the top also needs to be prepared with the addition of the blackwood decorative insert. This is set into the backpiece around $1/4$" (5mm). The backpiece is simply clamped and glued in place.

Polishing

This table was first sealed with shellac, which tends to even the color of the timber. Lacquer was then sprayed and cut between coats.

Dowelling jig used to drill holes in drawer sides.

Drilling holes for dowels on drawer back using drill press.

QTY	COMPONENT	LENGTH	WIDTH	THICKNESS
1	table top	$44^7/_8$ (1140)	17 (435)	$3/_4$ (20)
4	legs	$29^1/_2$ (750)	3 (75)	3 (75)
1	back piece	$31^1/_2$ (800)	1 (25)	$3/_4$ (20)
2	front rails	$31^1/_2$ (800)	2 (50)	$3/_4$ (20)*
2	side rails	$12^1/_4$ (310)	$5^3/_8$ (136)	$3/_4$ (20)*
1	back rail	$31^1/_2$ (800)	$5^3/_8$ (136)	$3/_4$ (20)*
1	vertical drawer divider	$3^3/_4$ (95)	2 (50)	$3/_4$ (20)
2	drawer fronts	$14^3/_4$ (375)	$3^3/_4$ (95)	$3/_4$ (20)

CUTTING LIST

Measurements in inches/mm
*plus tenons

Internal drawer runners and guides are measured and cut from final external dimensions.

A TABLE WITH FLARE

Hidden Drawer Table

Dovetailed, detailed and with a camouflaged drawer handle, this project will help develop beginner to intermediate woodworking skills.

Small tables are a popular request for the furniture maker, and may be required for 'occasional' use or a fixed purpose such as a bedside utility. I've made many variants of these over the years and standardised the measurements I generally make them to. The size, style, proportions, materials and joinery of this table are open to wide interpretation, but as a learning exercise the following project plan should get you started.

Here I've used some very dark pieces of one of my favourite woods, blackwood (*Acacia melanoxylon*), sourced direct from Tasmania. The front and side rails are dovetailed into the tops of the legs and panels sit between the side rails and legs. The drawer front, back and side panels all have a small vertically positioned moulding. On the drawer front this acts as a handle, creating a slight surprise as the front 'conceals' a drawer. The lower rails use a small mortise and tenon. The back is a standard one-piece rail.

First steps

After drawing a plan for the table I created a cutting list. Selecting several lengths of timber to cut my components from I looked for pieces that matched each other in color and grain and then decided which pieces looked best for the top, legs, panels and drawer front.

Legs

The legs are $1^7/_8$ x $1^7/_8$" (42 x 42mm) square. I didn't have any wood of this thickness so I had to glue timber together. **Photo 1** shows how dressed sections were glued and clamped together to achieve this thickness. When the glue had dried I machined the blanks square. At this time I also machined the rails and back and sawed everything to length.

Rail joints

A dovetail joint has two mating parts, a tail and a pin. **Photos 2, 3** and **4** show the sequence for cutting tails on the top front and side rails. A small rebate was cut in first on the router table **(photo 2)** in order to reduce the thickness of the dovetail and add a shoulder to the joint. The dovetail was then marked and sawn. A sharp chisel cleaned up the shoulders. This dovetail extends $^7/_8$" (22mm).

Cut the pins by laying the tail over the end of the leg and marking where the recess needs to go. I used a knife to mark this. I handsawed on the line **(photo 5)** and then drilled out some of the waste **(photo 6)**. A couple of chisels were used to clean up the recess **(photo 7).**

Check the fit **(photo 8),** making sure the shoulder meets the leg cleanly. The arrows are my working marks so I don't mix things up.

The top of the front legs receive two dovetails. These were cut away prior to assembly **(photo 9)**. The lower rails use a single mortise and tenon. In this case I marked the mortise first with two gauges **(photo 10).** I usually size these by eye, in this case they are around $^3/_4$ x $^9/_{16}$" (20 x 14mm) and $^7/_8$" (22mm) deep. Once again I drilled out the waste and then opened the hole with a chisel **(photo 11).**

Panels

The side panels are solid timber, $^3/_8$" (10mm) thick. They are housed in grooves in the legs and rails that were milled on the router table in no time at all **(photo 12)**.

The back uses one large mortise and tenon (left in **photo 13**). The tenon was cut on the router table and tablesaw, while the drill press and a chisel were used to make the mortise.

Once all components have been sanded the sides of the table can now be glued together. Check the legs are parallel with each other with no twist.

The side rail dovetails intersect into the front dovetail recess. The recess for the front rail dovetail pin needs to be opened up again by removing part of the side dovetail **(photo 14)**.

After the clamps are removed from the glued up side assemblies, the inner edge of the side rails may need to be planed level with the legs and any glue runs cleaned up. The front and back can now be glued to the sides. Work hard here to ensure the opening of the drawer is as square as possible and the inside of the table is square **(photo 15)**.

The drawer runners are machined ³/₄" x ³/₄" (20 x 20mm), sawn to length and then drilled and countersunk (photo 16). In **photo 17** the runners have been screwed and glued in place. The top kickers are treated in the same manner. The drawer guides were also glued in place **(photo 18)**. You can secure these by screwing them from below, that is, drilling through the bottom of the lower rail.

Now is a good time to glue the top together. In this case I used two wide boards to achieve full width **(photo 19)**.

The drawer

The drawer can now be made. I used Huon pine sides and back. The front joint is a large half blind dovetail with the addition of two walnut Miller dowels. The drawer sides and back are joined also with Miller dowels, while the drawer base is solid Huon rebated on three sides to fit into grooves in the drawer front and sides. I used to make little wood stops as drawer stops. I used to glue and tack these in place with brass

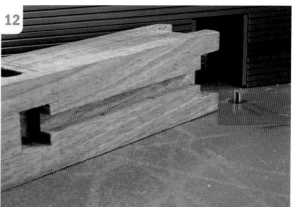

pins. I even tried screws and over the years I found that they seemed to always come loose. In this case I measured the drawer depth to exactly where I wanted the drawer to stop so that the back rail acts as a drawer stop.

The vertical moulds on the center of the side panels and the drawer front are all made from a length of wood ³/₄" (19mm) thick. The piece that functions as a drawer handle **(photo 20)** is rebated on two sides to fit into a groove in the drawer front.

HIDDEN DRAWER TABLE

The groove in the drawer front was once again milled on the router table. The drawer handle piece was cut well overlength so that cutting the rebate was easy and safe. I used a rebate plane for this in preference to milling such a small piece of wood on the router table. The vertical pieces on the sides were cut to length and glued in place after which I drilled holes for small locating dowels to be inserted.

The top has a large cove milled on the front and ends. Without this the top appeared to be far too heavy and thick for a small table. I cut the cove on the router table as well. The top is attached to the table with wooden table buttons. Everything was sanded again but with the intention to leave the edges crisp, particularly around the edge of the drawer.

I sanded up to 320 grit then applied three coats of oil over a period of six days. The table was then waxed and buffed to a low sheen.

CUTTING LIST		Measurements in inches/mm		
QTY	COMPONENT	LENGTH	WIDTH	THICKNESS
1	top	19 (480)	14¹/₄ (360)	⁷/₈ (22)
4	legs	19³/₄ (500)	1³/₄ (42)	1³/₄ (42)
2	front rails*	13 (330)	1³/₄ (42)	⁷/₈ (22)
4	side rails*	10³/₈ (265)	1³/₄ (42)	⁷/₈ (22)
1	back*	12 (330)	5¹/₄ (134)	⁷/₈ (22)
2	side panels	11¹/₄ (285)	4¹/₄ (110)	³/₈ (10)
4	drawer runners/kickers	11 (280)	⁷/₈ (22)	⁷/₈ (22)
2	drawer guides	10¹/₂ (265)	⁷/₈ (22)	¹/₂ (12)
1	drawer front	13 (330)	3¹/₂ (90)	⁷/₈ (22)
2	drawer sides	11⁷/₈ (298)	3¹/₂ (90)	¹/₂ (12)
1	drawer back	12 (305)	3 (75)	¹/₂ (12)
1	drawer base	12³/₈ (313)	11¹/₄ (286)	⁵/₁₆ (8)

*Note: Add allowance for dovetails and tenons

Hidden Drawer Desk

Vertical drawer pulls and bookmatched veneered leg faces feature on this blackwood desk.

The desk or hall table shown here has a similar theme to the Small Side Table, but I made some changes to the legs, curving them outward. If you don't want to go to the trouble of making curved legs you can of course keep them straight. The ultimate would be to steam bend the curves.

When I think about it, in some ways I used to just throw things together. The resulting random grain pattern on drawer faces and legs was how I just 'let the wood be itself' or a similar kind of justification. Now I realise how important selection of grain is. Using the grain or choosing specific grain for a certain part of a piece is critical.

Curved and grain matched legs

For the legs I wanted grain that would flow in the same direction as the curve. Finding one piece of wood with the right grain that could then be laminated onto the leg stock and then ripped into 'bookmatched' faces seemed to be the solution.

I first made a plywood template of the leg in the shape I wanted. The four pieces of $2^3/_4$ x $1^3/_4$" (70 x 42mm) blackwood set aside for the legs were cleaned up on the planer in preparation for gluing on the faces.

I spent quite a bit of time looking for a piece of blackwood with grain that

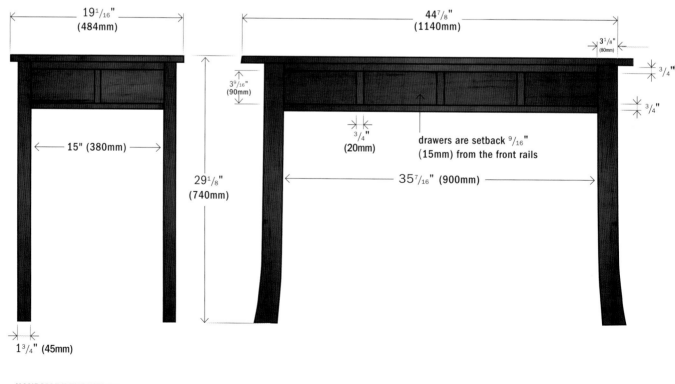

19$^1/_{16}$" (484mm)

44$^7/_8$" (1140mm)

3$^1/_8$" (80mm)

3$^9/_{16}$" (90mm)

$^3/_4$"

$^3/_4$"

15" (380mm)

$^3/_4$" (20mm)

drawers are setback $^9/_{16}$" (15mm) from the front rails

29$^1/_8$" (740mm)

35$^7/_{16}$" (900mm)

1$^3/_4$" (45mm)

1

Each leg has a bookmatched face laminated to it.

2

The small twin tenons on the rails.

3

Handsawing tenons on the lower rails. I use a saw guide that has a magnet which guides the blade for greater accuracy.

4

Showing overlapped dovetails and twin mortise and tenon joints.

curved the way I wanted. Predictably it wasn't till I had been through the whole stack that I found 'the one'. Of course the grain wasn't a perfect match to the curve, but by tilting the template and cutting slightly across the grain I was able to match the grain direction fairly closely to the outflowing curve of the legs.

I glued up two 'sandwiches', each consisting of two pieces of the leg stock with a 2³/₄" wide x ³/₄" thick (70mm x 20mm) piece of the 'special' wood in the middle. After drying overnight the clamps came off and the two laminated blocks were ripped lengthwise down the center filling to give four legs with glued-on bookmatched faces **(photo 1)**.

The legs could then be cleaned up, but plane the glued on faces first, removing as little material as possible. If you take off too much the grain pattern will change, spoiling the effect. The back can then be thicknessed to give 1³/₄"(45mm) total thickness. Once this was done it was a simple matter to position the template on each leg and carefully bandsaw the curves.

Rail to leg joints

The front and side rails for the desk are fitted on the flat to the legs. As the lower rails are only $1\frac{3}{4}$" x $\frac{3}{4}$"(42 x 20mm) a small joint is needed for the connection. Dowels or dominos can be used for the joint however the traditional joint to use for this application is a small twin mortise and tenon (**photos 2, 3**).

The front upper rail is dovetailed into the top of the legs. In this case I have also dovetailed the side rails into the tops of the legs. **Photo 4** shows how I deal with these partially 'overlapping' dovetails that were also explained in the Small Side Table project on p.24. The rear rail is $5\frac{1}{8}$"(130mm) wide and can be tenoned, dowelled or dominoed into the back legs. **Photos 5, 6, 7** show the steps.

Gluing up the frame

Solid wood panels are set into grooves routed into the legs and rails. A small piece of wood set in vertically gives the panelled look. Each vertical piece is $\frac{3}{4}$" wide and $\frac{3}{8}$"(20mm x 10mm)thick, and is fixed to the rails, not the panels. The sides were glued up first (**photo 8**) and then the front and back glued together.

In the photo showing the main glue-up (**photo 9**) you can see how the center runners and kicker are positioned. The drawer runners and guides can then be fitted.

The mortises for the back rail tenons are drilled and then cleaned out with a chisel.

If you do it right it will fit without force.

Marking out for one large back rail tenon.

The sides are glued up first.

The desk front and back are glued to the sides. Note how the center drawer runner and kicker are glued in at the same time.

CUTTING LIST

Measurements in inches/millimetres

QTY	COMPONENT	LENGTH	WIDTH	THICKNESS
1	top	45 (1140)	19 (484)	³/₄ (20)
2	side panels (approx)	15³/₄ (400)	14³/₈ (110)	³/₈ (10)
4	legs	28¹/₂ (720)	2³/₄ (70)	1³/₄ (45)
2	front rails*	35¹/₂ (900)	1¹/₂ (40)	³/₄ (20)
4	side rails*	15 (380)	1¹/₂ (40)	³/₄ (20)
1	back rail*	35¹/₂ (900)	5¹/₈ (130)	³/₄ (20)
	Drawers			
2	center runners/kickers	15 (380)	1¹/₂ (40)	³/₄ (20)
4	drawer runners/kickers	15 (380)	³/₄ (20)	³/₄ (20)
	drawer guides *as required*			
1	drawer front (cut into two)	35¹/₂ (900)	3¹/₂ (90)	³/₄ (20)
4	drawer sides (approx)	15³/₄ (400)	3¹/₂ (90)	¹/₂ (12)
2	drawer backs (approx)	16³/₈ (416)	3 (75)	¹/₂ (12)
2	drawer bases	15³/₄ (400)	16¹/₄ (416)	¹/₈ (3)
4	drawer slips	15 (380)	⁵/₁₆ (8)	⁵/₁₆ (8)
4	drawer pulls/mouldings	cut to fit	³/₄ (20)	⁵/₈ (15)

Note: Add allowance for dovetails and tenons

The top

I had two wide backsawn boards set aside for the top and glued them up with the rings of one facing up and the other down. The top has a 3¹/₈" (80mm) long overhang on the sides and sits ³/₄" (20mm) wider than the front. With only one join to make you'll glue this up in no time. I routed a 45° undercut on the lower edge of the top. When dry, sand or scrape the surface smooth before fitting the top to the frame with table buttons.

Drawers

The drawers have blackwood fronts but have Huon pine sides and blackwood ply bases. The bases are secured with slips rather than fitted into grooves. Handcut dovetails connect the drawer fronts and sides while Miller dowels were used to secure the backs. The vertical piece used as a drawer pull is slightly housed into the drawer front. After a final sand the desk was polished with shellac and wax.

Turned Leg Hall Table

A simple to make hall table with turned details.

The design for this blackwood table was arrived at after looking at some 18th century hall or 'pier' tables in an antique guide. The tables in the guide were much more ornate but all featured at least two turned legs and had lower rails that sat or almost sat on the floor. All permitted access for standing or sitting close to at the front. You could also add to the functionality of this design by incorporating a shelf.

I designed this piece as an exercise for a starting out maker so the construction is intentionally straightforward. Dowel joints were chosen as these are the simplest to make. They are time-proven in use and offer sufficient strength for this purpose. The turned coves and beads on the legs and the beading routed into the edges of the rails and top adds interest to a basic structure. You can buy pre-turned legs or turn your own if you wish.

At 3 1/2" (90mm) the lower rails are cut a little wider than the 3 1/8" (80mm) wide upper rails. The slight weighting of the lower rail adds visual balance.

Mark twice, cut once

This table is not difficult to make but you will come unstuck if you don't pay attention to a few key areas. Decide which piece of wood best suits the legs, rails or top. Check for the most pleasing arrangement of grain, especially for the top. Accuracy is crucial: pay close attention to measuring, marking out and machining and your chances of success are high. If your measurements and marks are 'only' a half a millimetre or so out these will compound, resulting in components that won't glue up square. Give thought to the details and edge treatments you use—it will look better if there's some consistency. If you're not experienced do some test joints, sample edge detailings first.

Prepare the legs

Four lengths of Tasmanian blackwood $1\frac{7}{8}$ x $1\frac{7}{8}$" (60 x 60mm) square were machined and turned **(photo 1)**. The legs are 30" (760mm) long and feature coves and beads on each end, connected by a tapered column.

The details of the leg were crisply turned to minimise sanding—oversanding details and edges will detract from the look of the finished piece **(photo 2)**.

Prepare the joints

Before any jointing can be carried out on the legs they need to be arranged to the best display of grain pattern **(photo 3)**. If there are any defects position them so they face the rear of the piece. The rails were planed and thicknessed, and

then sawn to length on the miter saw **(photo 4)**.

A basic store-bought dowelling jig was used to drill the holes in the ends of the rails **(photo 5)**. Despite its low cost this jig works well, provided you take care to accurately match the dowels to the drill bit you use. Do some test holes in offcuts to make sure the dowels will fit snugly in the holes before you proceed to your machined components. If the dowels fit too tightly you'll risk splitting the wood. On the other hand if the fit is too sloppy your joints will result in a weak construction.

I used three dowels for each of the corner joints (eight for the upper frame, six for the lower). I marked off $\frac{3}{4}$"(20mm), $1\frac{9}{16}$" (40mm) and $2\frac{1}{4}$" (60mm) lines on the end of the $2\frac{1}{4}$" (80mm) wide rail and $\frac{3}{4}$"

TURNED LEG HALL TABLE

(20 mm), 1³/₄" (45mm) and 2³/₄" (70mm) on the 3¹/₂" (90mm) rail). Using whole numbers for measuring simplifies things.

The legs were marked carefully before drilling for dowels (photo 6). I used a center punch to make a small depression that would help to locate the drill bit. The holes were then drilled on the drill press.

The beading can now be run on the edge of the rails. As shown in photo 7, I clamped an extra board to the workpiece to give more support for the laminate trimmer base to run on.

Sand components

With all the jointing completed the components can all be sanded before assembly (photo 8). A 'dry' test assembly before applying glue is highly recommended. I sanded with a belt sander to 120 grit and then moved to the random orbit, going to 150 grit.

Assembly

When gluing the frames together I place small blocks of wood between the component and the clamp head (photo 9). This avoids bruising the workpiece and lets me position the clamp so even pressure is applied. Check the components are glued up parallel by getting down at eye level with the workpiece and then sighting along the rails. Next measure the diagonals of the frame with a tape measure from one internal corner

to the other. If the measurements are not the same your frame is not square and you need to move the clamps to correct this. The clamps on the longest diagonal need to be adjusted by moving them in the same direction of the out-of-square distortion. Move the clamp and pressure block. Make small changes and keep checking the diagonals till you've got it right. If you've machined your wood square and cut all you components accu-

CUTTING LIST				Measurements in inches/mm * plus tenons
1	top	42¹/₄ (1070)	18 (460)	³/₄ (20)
2	upper rails	31¹/₄ (800)	3¹/₈ (80)	³/₄ (20)
2		12¹/₂ (320)	3¹/₈ (80)	³/₄ (20)
1	lower rails	31¹/₄ (800)	3¹/₂ (90)	³/₄ (20)
2		12¹/₂ (320)	3¹/₂ (90)	³/₄ (20)
4	legs	30 (760)	2¹/₄ (60)	2¹/₄ (60)

rately everything should go together easily. Even small inaccuracies will result in out-of-square problems. If you can't get the frame square you need to go back and recheck all measurements and angles, correcting if necessary.

The panel for the top was glued up from four boards, two wider and two thinner. Turned leg tables often have Roman ogee type profiles routed on their edges but I decided to use the same beading bit I had earlier used on the rails.

To attach the top, wood buttons were positioned into slots that were cut with a biscuit jointer. The buttons were then screwed to the top to hold it in place but still allow for timber movement. The large corner blocks shown in **photo 10** strengthen the joints by triangulation. These are glued and screwed in place.

Finishing

Polishing is one of the most important processes in making any piece. Here I decided to use a shellac and wax finish. Sanding is very important and I went up to 1200 grit. I first used the belt sander using 100 grit, then the random orbit sander with 120 and 150 grit. After this it was all hand sanding, working up through 180, 220, 320, 400, 600 and finally 1200 grit.

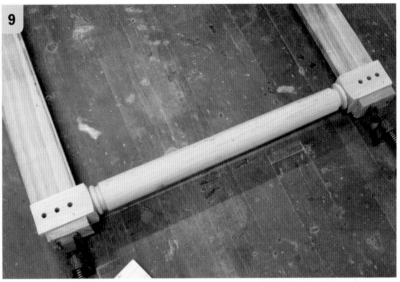

Shellac is a great polish to use as it evens out the coloring between different pieces of wood. A ready mixed gold shellac was diluted about 50% for the first coat. After that two more coats were applied with a quality brush, sanding with 1200 grit between coats. After the final coat had dried overnight I sanded again with 1200 grit and applied a hard wax. The wax is easy to use as long as you apply it sparingly to small areas at a time and buff straight away. It's all about wax on, wax off.

Blackwood Bedside Tables

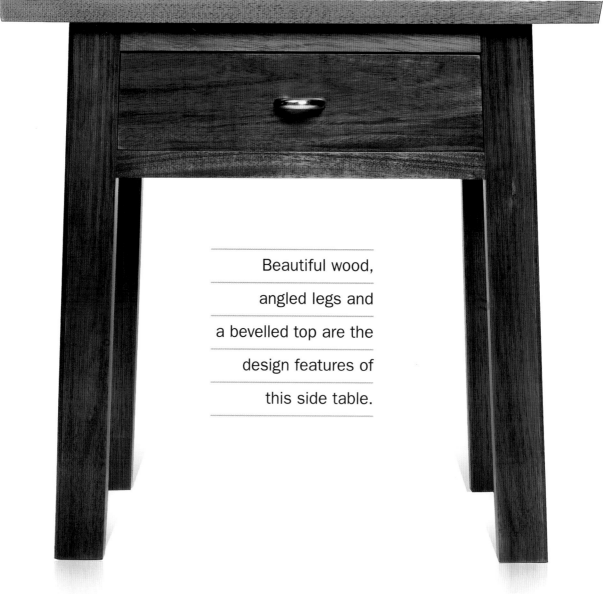

Beautiful wood,

angled legs and

a bevelled top are the

design features of

this side table.

Bedside tables are in my opinion a very expensive item. By this I mean they cost a maker more to make in terms of time and skill required than, say, a table. They have as many joints as a larger piece like a cabinet does, but the reduced scale means a more demanding level of skill is needed for joints and components. If you're making for a paying client you have to carefully consider how to price a piece that is labour intensive but has only a small physical size. Most customers want to see where their money is going and bigger can initially seem like a lot more. Fine timber, detailing and design are the points that furniture makers need to capitalise on.

Design inspiration

There is some Chinese inspiration with this design. A traditional Chinese small table might have had angled legs, a bead running around the faces of the drawer frame and heavily profiled leg edges. The top might also have had an upsweeping breadboard end. All these features require a very high level of skill and time to complete. The bedside tables don't follow this formula but borrow the idea of angled legs. The legs are rounded on their outer edges and the top, while without an uplift, has a gentle bevel on its side and front edges. Even though the legs are angled, the construction of the table is quite simple.

I had to base some of my design decisions on the budget that was allowed for the piece. The main features of the table are its overall form and functionality, and the timber itself. I used one of my favourite species, Tasmanian blackwood. Other Australian timber choices could include jarrah, NSW rosewood, Qld maple or even redgum.

Dimensions

A height of $19^3/_4$" (500mm) or so will suit most beds, while length needs to be less than $23^5/_8$" (600mm) and depth around 15" (380mm). I spent some time working out my measurements then made a full size drawing on some cardboard to get more of the feel. From this I established my component widths and thicknesses **(photo 1)**. I next selected and dressed the wood but left it overlength for final sawing later.

I then made a kind of mock-up to get a 'real' idea of the look of the tables **(photo 2)**. I used masking tape to hold parts together and so I could visualise what different overhangs would look like. Once the final

Cutting Twin Mortise and Tenons

A The lower front rail can use a twin mortise and tenon.

B Handsawing at a small scale like this is good training. For the first cut I clamped a piece of wood as a guide and used a fine Japanese saw to saw cross grain.

C The Japanese saw was not as effective for ripping. I found a western style saw much better for this.

D The remaining waste was drilled and chiselled out.

lengths of the components were decided these could be sawn to length and the jointing started.

Rounding the legs

The outer edges of each leg were rounded in two stages. First a rounding-over bit in the laminate trimmer gave the basic shape. The outermost edge was then shaped a bit more with a handplane.

Cut to length

The essence of this design is the angle the legs splay out at. I settled on 2.5°. With the miter saw set at this angle the legs can be cut **(photo 3)**. Look hard at the wood you are using and decide which face best has the grain pattern in harmony with the angle the leg sits at. You want to avoid grain that runs the opposite way. At a minimum have the grain running parallel. Use a stop

block on the miter saw fence so that all legs are identical in length. Leave the angle set on the miter saw.

Now for the front and rear rails. Note the top front rail is shorter than its lower counterpart. To establish this measurement first determine where the lower rail will sit. I have it so that the drawer opening is 3½" (90mm). Use a bevel gauge set at 2.5° to pencil in the position on the leg and allow for the thickness of the two rails. The length of the rails will vary depending on the joinery you use. For dowels or loose tenons the rails are cut to the opening size, but for traditional mortise and tenon add on the length of the tenon. Sawing at 2.5° (that's why you leave the angle set from sawing the legs) cut the two lower rails (I was making two tables). With the stop block in the same position cut the two back rails now **(photo 4)**.

Take one lower rail and lay it and two legs on a bench in final position. Lightly clamp the rail. You can directly establish a length for the top rail now and saw it to length (**photo 5** shows the rail and side). The two side rails are sawn at the 90° so there are no issues here in measuring.

After sawing you can't assume the cuts are clean and will mate properly. I checked and needed to lightly trim the ends of wider rails with a plane **(photo 6)**.

The joints

The front rails are the trickiest. There are a couple of options: dovetail the top one into the top of the leg and use twin mortise and tenons on the lower rail, or use dominos or dowels. The back rails can be tenoned or dowelled.

Remember the wood on the front and back rails is angled and tenons or dowels need to be angled at 2.5° so the joint between it and the leg is horizontal. If you were using dowels for example, cut a sliver of wood at 2.5° and place it between the dowel jig base and the end grain of the wood so you can bring the dowel hole horizontal. You can use a similar technique for loose tenons or dominos.

The joints on the side rails are straightforward, no angle is needed. Mortise and tenons or dowels are the norm for these joints. Where the top edge of the side rail meets the top of the legs (which are at 2.5°) it extends past the top of the leg. I planed this flush much later in the making process. I left the lower edge at 90° as it is completely hidden from view.

Glue-up

The fronts and backs were glued up first. Use angled cauls under the clamp heads to bring the rails together horizontally. The sides are glued in place and it is important at this stage to check there is no twist in the assembly. Placing the assembly on a flat surface will show you if there is twist. After the glue has dried some planing will inevitably be needed to flush the rails to the legs **(photo 7).**

The table frame can now be glued up and needs to be square. If the measurement between corners is the same it is square **(photo 8)**. (See over the page for three ways of doing this.)

Drawer guides

Inside the assembly the drawer runners, kickers and guides now need to be fitted. One edge of the runners and kickers is sawn at 2.5°, then glued and screwed to the inside of the side rails **(photo 9)**. As their name suggests the drawer guides lead the drawer into the cavity.

Spend some time ensuring they are glued in parallel **(photo 10)**.

The drawers

These have blackwood fronts with Huon pine sides and back. The front joint is what I call my 'raf special' where I use one large dovetail and two dowels, while the rear uses dowels only. It's not as good as traditional dovetails, but it is faster and still has much of the strength and appeal. As the drawer front is sawn to 2.5° I make the sides a little wider so the edges extend past the front edges. The excess wood is planed flush with the front later **(photo 11)**. Once again, check all is square.

Making the top

Three boards were glued up to make the width of the top. I used wood from the same board to keep the color and grain consistent. The amount of overhang at the sides was carefully considered. What you see is my result but you may wish to have less overhang. Note the angle cut on the underside of the top is about 15°. The top is secured to the table frame with wood buttons **(photo 12)**.

The handles are a critical part of any piece. My choice for these tables was modern solid brass pulls. Perhaps a little large but it seems to work.

Applying a finish

Polishing is a separate process and I ended up sending these tables to a french polisher who applied a shellac and wax finish. The shellac tends to even out the color of the blackwood as well as sealing the wood. The wax is a renewable top coat that gives a low sheen and silky feel that people like.

Setting the legs at an angle adds an element of complexity to making this piece, however with careful planning and accurate measuring and marking you'll be able to achieve a good result.

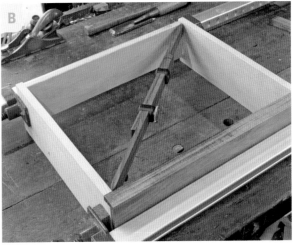

Three ways to check for square

Making sure your work is glued up square is essential. Here are three ways to check your work is on the mark.

A Simplest, cheapest and slowest, although just as good, is a steel rule.

B A sliding bar gauge is a fast way to get your work square. The one shown is made up from a Veritas fitting and wood sections that you supply yourself.

C Use a large square—this can be a manufactured one or else shop-made.

QTY	COMPONENT	LENGTH	WIDTH	THICKNESS
CUTTING LIST				*Measurements in inches/mm*
1	top	22 (560)	14¹/₂ (370)	⁷/₈ (21)
4	legs	19³/₄ (500)	2 (50)	1¹/₄ (32)
2	front rails (minimum) *	13³/₄ (350)	1¹/₄ (32)	⁷/₈ (22)
2	side rails*	10³/₄ (275)	5¹/₂ (140)	1 (25)
1	back (angled)*	13³/₄ (350)	5³/₈ (138)	1 (25)
4	drawer runners (kickers	10³/₄ (275)	1¹/₄ (30)	1 (25)
2	drawer guides	10³/₄ (275)	¹/₂ (14)	¹/₂ (14)
1	drawer front	13³/₄ (350)	3¹/₂ (90)	⁷/₈ (22)
2	drawer sides	11³/₄ (300)	3¹/₂ (90)	¹/₂ (12)
1	drawer back	12³/₄ (325)	2³/₄ (70)	¹/₂ (12)
1	drawer base	12 (302)	11¹/₂ (290)	³/₁₆ (4)
2	drawer slips	11¹/₄ (285)	⁵/₈ (15)	³/₈ (10)

Note: Add allowance for dovetails and tenons

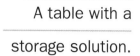

Wine Table

At first glance this piece is a simple hall table, but it has a small secret. The top is hinged and lifts to reveal a storage space that comfortably holds six bottles of wine. The build is no more than a traditional table with four legs, four rails and a top.

The four legs are arranged to best display the grain pattern **(photo 1)**. You need to avoid bad grain layout such as short grain at the ends or too bold a swirl. If the grain runs off at the foot of a leg it looks really bad. In this case the front legs (on top in the photo) are built up from two laminations with the front facing side bookmatched. The grain pattern of the light colored Douglas fir is quite low key, but the bookmatching improves the look.

The four rails can be joined to the legs with dowels, tenons or dominos—your choice. In **photo 2** I am marking the joint locations. I mark one rail and then bring this up to the mating leg. This rail becomes the template used to mark the other components. If you use a ruler to mark everything separately it is slower and not as accurate.

Photo 3 shows most of the components with all the joints made. I am using floating mortise and tenon joints. I have no problem with using dowels in this application or you could make hand cut mortise and tenons.

With the joints made the fronts and back rails can be glued to the legs **(photo 4)**. Check there is no twist—sight along the wood to ensure the two legs are parallel. If not you can apply a twist and/or pack up one clamp at a corner. The next glue-up is to join the sides to the front and back. The front and back are joined and the lower rails are also glued at the same time.

With the frame complete I mocked up various wood pieces until I was happy with the final dimensions of the top and mouldings and their overhangs. The mouldings are small $3/4$"x $3/4$" (20 x 20mm) square section wood. They are glued onto the lower edge of the rails and are purely decorative.

The mouldings are checked out at the corners to wrap around the legs and meet at a miter. The check-out was mostly cut on the tablesaw **(photo 5)** with cleaning up and final fitting completed with a chisel. You can also use a router for this process.

Resting on the top of the frame in **photo 6** you can see one of these with the check-out complete, note the miter at the ends. Below that you can see how one of the moulds has been glued and clamped on. These mouldings all needed to be individually fitted as the gap between the outside of the leg and the rail face varied a little. No matter how careful you are with machining joints there

CUTTING LIST				Measurements in inches/mm
QTY	COMPONENT	LENGTH	WIDTH	THICKNESS
1	legs	19 (480)	$1^1/_2$ (40)	$1^1/_2$ (40)
2	rails	$20^7/_8$ (530)	5 (125)	$3/_4$ (20)
		$12^1/_4$ (310)	5 (125)	$3/_4$ (20)
2	lower side rails	$12^1/_4$ (310)	$1^3/_4$ (45)	$3/_4$ (20)
1	lower long rail	22 (550)	$1^3/_4$ (45)	$3/_4$ (20)
2	mouldings	$16^1/_8$ (410)	$3/_4$ (20)	$3/_4$ (20)
		$24^7/_8$ (630)	$3/_4$ (20)	$3/_4$ (20)
2	top frame	$27^1/_2$ (700)	$1^3/_4$ (45)	$3/_4$ (20)
		$16^1/_2$ (420)	$1^3/_4$ (45)	$3/_4$ (20)
		13 (330)	$1^3/_4$ (45)	$3/_4$ (20)
2	internal support cleats	22 (550)	$3/_4$ (20)	$3/_4$ (20)
		13 (330)	$3/_4$ (20)	$3/_4$ (20)
1	internal support cleats	13 (330)	$1^1/_2$ (40)	$3/_4$ (20)
1	internal felt covered panel plywood	22 (550)	13 (330)	$3/_{16}$ (4)
2	hinges			
1	brass stay			

*Note: Add allowance for dovetails and tenons

is usually some variation in the final joints, hopefully no more than $1/64$" (half a millimetre).

The top is a frame and panel construction. The framing timber has a groove cut in the middle to accept the panel. The frame timber should be sawn overlength at this stage. The groove can be made using a router, or as I have done on the tablesaw, where I made a series of cuts to achieve the $3/8$" wide x $1/4$" deep (10mm x 6mm) deep groove I wanted.

The groove formed on a tablesaw needed to be cleaned up. I used a chisel (photo 7) but for hand tool lovers a narrow shoulder plane is an alternative and elegant tool of choice. Either way you need to end up with a groove that has an even width and depth.

The panels for the top were glued from all the remaining bits of dry Douglas fir I had left in the shed. I played around with the grain layout but was pushed because there was barely enough wood to use. When I was happy with the layout I pencilled a large triangle on the wood (photo 8). This traditional form of marking helps keep track of the board arrangement.

Each panel was glued up individually (photo 9). The Japanese clamps I'm using are solid brass and because they are light are great for small glue-ups like this. I've had a few of these clamps for over 25 years and they are still fine.

The frame pieces were cut to final length on the miter saw (photo 10). I cut the outside pieces and then worked out the length of the three internal pieces. Photo 11 shows how the corner joints go together. The mortise in the end grain can be seen as can the groove to accept the panel.

Unfortunately I left off choosing the hinges until later so I found myself without the correct hinge solution—you can learn from my mistake here. The hinge I did use was eventually sourced via the internet. It is a table flap hinge which I reversed, that is I used the inside for the face which necessitated the countersinking of the screw holes on the face and polishing the brass (photo 12). I have to admit that I got lucky with the hinges. I made the legs $1^{19}/_{32}$" (40mm) square and the hinge I bought is $1^{17}/_{32}$" (39mm) wide. The moral is to try and plan final details of a piece through to the end, especially bought-in components like hardware.

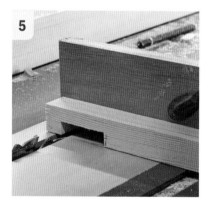

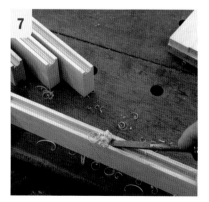

Finishing

A wood like Douglas fir can be planed instead of sanded. All timber should be planed prior to glue-up. I still sanded some components though as the panels, for instance, were easier to smooth this way. Your choice of polish can be shellac, lacquer, or oil and wax.

I designed the compartment under the top to hold seven bottles of wine. You should check this measurement against your own bottle stash.

Low Table

The round legs on this coffee

table are planed, not turned.

This simple design is one that I have made a lot of variations of over the years, and the round leg is the main feature. The rail to leg joint is a mortise and tenon which is reasonably straightforward to make. A flat area needs to be made to accept the rail and this is planed in before the leg is rounded. The leg can be turned on a lathe and this will give a superior finish. If you don't have a lathe, or simply want to master the skill of planing wood to round you can make the legs the way I did. Planing the legs will give facets to the leg surface. You can leave this as a detail or you can fine sand the legs to a smooth finish. After the legs were planed round I used a v-chisel to carve in a groove near the base of the legs. The top was glued up from five boards and fine sanded. The edge treatment of the top was to ease over the corners with a handplane. With such a simple design there's a lot of scope for variations. You could use contrasting timbers or inlays, or decorate the top with carved motifs or wood burnings.

The wood in this project was supplied square dressed so my first step was to saw all the components to length. Remember that the rails need to be sawn to allow extra length for the tenons.

1

Mark out where the mortises will be placed. They are centered in the leg and only the upper and lower borders need to be marked.

2

The mortise is cut with a spiral cutter in the router. The router is set up with its fence in place. Holding the workpiece in the vice, the router is plunged down and moved along to create the mortise. It's best to make the mortise with a couple of passes.

3

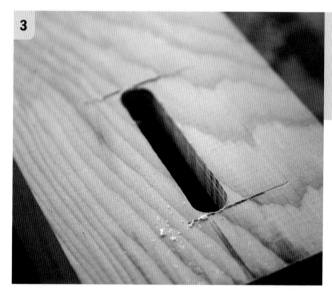

This is a completed mortise. Note that the length of the mortise is achieved by visually stopping the router at the pencil line. If you were making a batch of tables then it would be worthwhile to make up a jig that would define the length of the mortise.

4

CUTTING LIST *Measurements in inches/mm*
* plus tenons

QTY	COMPONENT	LENGTH	WIDTH	THICKNESS
5	**top**	45$^{1}/_{2}$ (1155)	4$^{3}/_{4}$ (120)	$^{3}/_{4}$ (19)
2	**rails***	34$^{1}/_{4}$ (870)	3$^{1}/_{8}$ (80)	$^{3}/_{4}$ (19)
2	**rails***	15$^{1}/_{2}$ (395)	3$^{1}/_{8}$ (80)	$^{3}/_{4}$ (19)
4	**legs**	17 (430)	2$^{1}/_{2}$ (65)	$^{3}/_{4}$ (19)

A large flat area now needs to be machined into the legs. This is done on the planer. A stop is mounted on the outfeed table and the leg pushed forward to the stop. There may be some tear-out which can be cleaned up later.

5

The legs need to be rounded and without a lathe they need to be planed down. The leg on the left has had the flat planed in where the rail sits. I marked the centers on the leg ends before doing any planing.

6

Both marking and cutting gauges were used to define the shoulders and depth of the tenons. I have allowed the thickness of the tenon to be a fraction oversize so that it can be trimmed to fit the mortise—you can't put the wood back on if you take off too much.

7

If your tablesaw is accurate the shoulders can be sawn with it. The saw table has to be spot on otherwise the shoulders won't match. Sometimes I can't get my saw to cut accurately while on other days it is great.

8

The shoulders have all been sawn cleanly. More waste can be quickly removed by taking multiple cuts, leaving less waste for the laminate trimmer to remove.

9

A straight cutter in the laminate trimmer removes waste and should leave a neat flat area on the cheek of the tenon. To avoid disasters (how would I know about that?) I keep the trimmer cutting well clear of the shoulder.

10

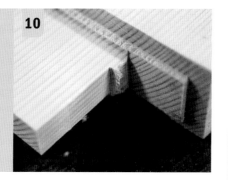

The chisel is needed here to clean up the corners and get everything square. I chop down first, creeping up to the line and making the first cuts angled away from the shoulder. The last cut should be 'perfectly' vertical.

11

It may sound obvious, but properly sharpened tools, like this chisel, will make a huge difference to your work.

The celery top pine is quite good to work. It is not soft at all but can be pared well, planing is okay but the grain can switch around quickly.

12

13

Now is the time to make the legs round. Without a lathe they can be planed to a pleasing round shape. Setting the planer fence to 45° allows the corners to be taken off. It is important to plane evenly along the length.

CELERY TOP PINE

Celery top pine *(Phyllocladus asplenifolius)* is the timber used for this project. It's native to Tasmania and mainly grows in the west of that state although there are some areas on the east coast where it grows. Although it's a tall-growing conifer it doesn't resemble a pine tree. It is more closely related to yew species and is distinguished by foliage that resembles the vegetable it's named after. It can grow to 40 metres in height and the oldest specimens of 400 years or so can achieve a diameter of 24 inches. The oldest living celery top pines are about 800 years old.

The photos of the coffee table made here will show you its attractive straw blonde color. This will mellow with age. The wood is hard, strong and dense and is stable in cross-section but can shrink longitudinally as it dries.

Traditionally it has been used for boatbuilding, joinery, flooring, panelling and furniture and it also turns well. The grain of celery top pine is usually straight and clear and, compared to darker timbers like blackwood, is very clean to work. Workability is good and celery top pine is reputed to be excellent for steam bending, however the frequent presence of compression wood can make it a little unpredictable. Because celery top pine is tasteless and odourless it is an excellent wood to make breadboards, serving platters and utensils from.

14

I used the power plane to remove waste, then turned to the hand plane. The celery top planes quite well and I tried to achieve the best finish possible. I kept the tool sharp by honing the blade after every leg.

15

The more time you spend the better the potential result. You can sand after the planing for a smoother finish or leave it straight off the plane which is what I did.

The leg and rail joint is complete and the rail has been sanded. Each joint will probably need tuning to get right. It is best to have the rail proud rather than below the end of the leg. This is because it will be easier to plane it flush rather than trying to plane the end of the leg flush with the rail.

16

17

Two clamps are used to bring the rails to the legs. The shaped block spreads the clamp pressure.

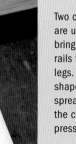

Final assembly

Once the table frame has been glued up it needs to be prepared for the top. Plane flush the rails to the leg ends and remove any glue runs. I attached the top to the rails with wood buttons. The slots for the buttons were cut by making multiple plunges with the biscuit joiner.

Reverse Taper Low Table

Changing the proportioning and
detailing of an otherwise plain
design can make a difference.

Many years ago I made a low table from blackwood for some friends. Recently I heard that they still liked the piece, so I was inspired to make a similar one, but with a few changes. That table had square legs and used the same system for the rails as the piece shown above.

Tapers and rails

For this table I decided to use a reverse taper leg, meaning the leg would taper upwards rather than in the more usual downward direction. Taper down legs

are a pretty standard leg design for many tables. They give a piece a lighter uplifting look. The reverse taper leg is a heavier look but also quite grounding, as it makes the table look as if it is firmly planted on the floor. I chose to use blackwood, one of my favourite timbers. Many timbers are suitable though, although I would suggest going for a darker color.

The rails are like a small ladder. The little vertical 'rungs' are evenly spaced along the long rails and tenoned or dowelled in place. The long rails are then tenoned into the legs. As the leg to rail joint is potentially a weak point I took care to make these

tenons as long as possible and made sure the fit was good. To add strength an internal bracing angle block was glued and screwed in place later in the making.

The rail sections are made from $1^{1}/_{4}$" (32mm) square wood. Actually I didn't have any timber that size so I laminated up that size from 1" (25mm) sawn timber. I glued up wide sections and then ripped these over-size before planing and thicknessing to the desired $1^{1}/_{4}$" (32mm). After all the joints have been made the small vertical rungs are planed down to about $1^{1}/_{8}$" (29mm) on the face side. The fact they are slightly thinner creates a nice shadow line where they meet the long rails. Details add to the look of an otherwise plain piece like this.

A good framework

Frame assembly is best done by gluing the long sides up first. I used dominos for the mortise and tenons. I find that these can be manufactured a little too wide to fit the mortise neatly hence I plane the

Tapering the legs

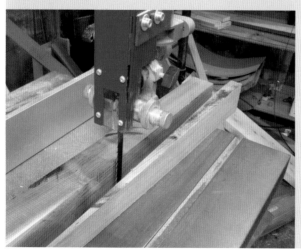

As with most woodworking operations there's more than one way to do this process. If you were doing production runs it would be worth taking the time to make up a jig, or you can buy a taper-cutting jig from a tool retailer. The one I have is shown left and made of light aluminium but is quite adequate for occasional use. The jig holds the wood at an angle to the tablesaw blade and allows you to easily make repeatable cuts.

The legs are $2^{1}/_{2}$" (65mm) square at the base and taper up to 2" (50mm) at the top. The taper is applied only to the two outside faces. The two inside faces are left square and straight. All measurements are taken using these square faces as a reference.

Once the legs have been sawn to length the taper can be made.

Mark the tops and bottoms of each leg and then draw a line on the wood on one outside face measuring from one corner to the other. Cut the taper on the tablesaw (**left above**) or on the bandsaw (**left**). Draw the taper line on the other outside face and cut that the same way.

The sawn faces will need to be cleaned up either with a machine or a hand plane. Keep the offcuts from sawing the taper, you'll need these later when gluing up the frame.

A final going-over with the handplane prior to assembly.

Legs, rails and 'rungs' for the table have now been cut and machined for domino joints.

The legs and long rails are glued and left overnight, then the frame can be assembled with the short rails. The offcuts from the taper cuts make perfectly angled glue blocks.

sides and fit them to each mortise. To do a test dry assembly I use some spare dominos that I take a hammer to and flatten slightly to make them a bit looser in the mortise. When I know that everything is well fitted I substitute new dominos, apply glue and clamp up the frames.

Before glue-up remember that with a fiddly table frame like this it is better to sand or fine plane the components before assembly. It is very difficult and time-consuming to do this after glue-up. I planed as much of the blackwood as possible but had to resort to the belt sander to smooth some of the rails. The grain, as is common with blackwood, was too wild for my planing skills and my patience.

The offcuts from sawing the taper now come into play for the glue-up. Saw some short pieces of these to use as cauls between the clamps and legs. They allow the clamps to pull everything together straight.

I like the upper rails to line up perfectly with the top of the legs. Because it's difficult to plane this joint level at a later stage I took time adjusting the dominos until I was happy with the fit. Some people argue it's better to have the rails sitting a tiny bit proud of the tops of the legs. The reasoning is that if the rails ever shrink in height they will end up level with the top of the legs and the top will still be flat. However if the rails were made level with the top initially and

then shrink at a later date, they would be below the top of the legs. The danger is the table top could cup, as it would be sitting on the top of the legs but lower in the middle. In this piece however the rails are narrow ($1^1/_4$"/32mm) and movement should never cause a problem.

Making and attaching the top

Five boards were machined and their edges jointed for the top. You can use biscuits to help bring the boards together if you wish. I made the middle board $5^1/_2$" (140mm) wide. This is because on the end rails the space between the two middle short rungs is $5^1/_2$". When the table is viewed from the ends it should all line up. There is a quite a long overhang on the top—5" (125mm) at the ends and $1^1/_2$" (37mm) at the sides.

The top is attached to the frame with traditional style wood buttons. When you place these buttons think about the prevailing weather conditions. If it's dry the top will be at its narrowest, hence it can in the future expand in width in wet weather. Placing the buttons away from the rail by $1/_{16}$" (2mm) or so will give the top some room to move in the future.

Bevelling the edge of the top

The top edge also has a bevel of 20°. To form this bevel I used an electric plane with an added wood sub-fence

Using the electric planer to bevel the top edges with the aid of a sub-fence that I machined up on the tablesaw to the angle I wanted.

sawn to the desired angle on the tablesaw. Using the plane with the fence formed a consistent bevel on the edges of the top.

The corners are rounded slightly to remove the sharp edge. I rounded the edges by hand with sandpaper. Actually I think that sharp edges can often look better, but people like furniture that is friendly.

One salesperson told me how she had a fantastic table on the gallery floor once. This piece was all hard and sharp angles resembling a 'stealth' bomber. It looked great but she gouged her leg on it one day and hated the table thereafter. There is also the danger of small children injuring themselves on sharp corners.

Your own style

You can use the basic proportions of this table and customise it to your own taste with more or less detailing as desired. Of course you may choose not to taper the legs. Making mock-ups and samples of different edgings or rail treatments can help you to sort out the effects you do and don't like before it's too late.

Traditional table buttons secure the top. A corner block braces the structure.

CUTTING LIST
Measurements in inches/mm

QTY	COMPONENT	LENGTH	WIDTH	THICKNESS
1	top (glued up from 5 boards)	49 (1240)	25⅞ (655)	¾ (20)
4	legs	16¼ (410)	2½ (65)	2½ (65)
4	rails (long)	36 (910)	1¼ (32)	1¼ (32)
4	rails (short)	19 (480)	1¼ (32)	1¼ (32)
12	rungs	3 (75)	1¼ (32)	1⅛ (28)

Applying a finish

Before polishing I sanded and planed everything as smooth as I could. Smooth is a relative term of course. I will happily go to 320 grit abrasive, working up from 100, 120, 180 and 240. Sometimes I throw in 150 grit after the 120. After the 320 grit paper I also burnished the surface by rubbing it with the back of the sandpaper. That treatment gives a fine finish that I find will accept oil or lacquers. Some makers will go up to 1200 grit or more. Even better.

I applied several coats of furniture oil over a period of a week. After this a hard wax was applied and buffed.

Splay Leg Dining Table

Angles, inlays and rail
supports add detail
to this medium-sized
dining table.

Splayed or angled out legs are the main feature of this design. Although there's some fiddling around with angles, it's really not too difficult to make. Once you understand the principle of creating joints at angles other than 90° you can apply this to your other designs.

The angles on this table are between the long rails and the legs—the short rails are joined at 90°. The tops and bottoms of the legs need to be cut at 2.5° (my chosen angle). **Photo 1** shows how I did this on the miter saw. I sawed the leg tops and bottoms, as well as the long rails in the one operation so only the one miter saw setting was used. There's less danger of inaccuracy this way. The short rails were sawn at 90° afterwards. A length stop on the miter saw table (**photo 2**) gave consistent results.

Before I docked the legs I looked at them carefully, deciding on the best possible grain orientation. It will look better if the grain flows in the direction of the angle rather than away from it.

Joints

On the long sides the rail to leg joint needs to allow for the joint being at an angle. Mortise and tenon, floating tenons (shop-made or dominos), or dowels can be used. If you use dominos or a dowelling jig, tape a sliver of wood sawn at 2.5° to the base of the domino tool or the jig to tilt the angle of cutting. **Photo 3** shows the mortise in the end of the 90° short rail.

Combining woods

I wanted to use a lighter colored wood for the base of the table so

I chose some Tasmanian celery top pine. The top was made from blackwood. To tie the top and base together I created blackwood 'feet' on the legs.

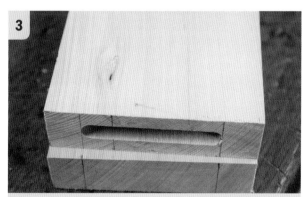

Sawing the rails to length.

Use a length stop for repeatable and accurate cuts.

Leg to rail joint, in this case a floating mortise and tenon.

Using a router plane to clean up the recess for the blackwood feet.

5

Sawing the blackwood trim on the bandsaw.

6

Gluing on the outside trim pieces.

7

Cleaning up to the shoulder with a chisel.

8

Applying the final trim pieces.

9

How the trim looks when finished.

10

The long sides were glued first.

11

Use angled glue blocks to clamp things up .

Making the 'feet'

A large step was routed on the end of each leg. I first made a cut on the tablesaw to define the shoulder and then ran the legs over a straight cutter on the router table to almost complete the machining. I routed almost to the pre-sawn shoulder then chiselled out the bulk of the waste before finishing with a router plane (**photo 4**). Router planes are great for simple work like this, and they are quiet.

The blackwood trim was sawn on the bandsaw (**photo 5**). I made it $^1/_{16}$" (2mm) thicker than the depth of the routed out face. Gluing the trim to each leg was a two-stage process. Opposing faces were glued (**photo 6**), and allowed to dry before the other sides were cleaned up (**photo 7**) and next glued (**photo 8**). When the glue was dry the trim was flushed off with the legs. You can see how it all goes together in **photo 9**)

Test assemble

With the legs prepared and the rails cut I then did a test assembly. As I was using loose tenons I prepared some of these that were, well…loose. The real tenons were made later and these were a neat snug fit. The 'loose' loose tenons were only used for test assembly so the table frame could be brought together to check the rails would be flush at the top.

After I was satisfied with everything the long sides were glued up (**photo 10**). Use angle blocks between the clamp and legs to align things parallel (**photo 11**). I leave glue-ups like these overnight to dry. The next

The short rails are glued in place and the whole frame checked for square.

day the short rails are glued in place to complete the making of the table frame…almost (**photo 12**).

Bevels and blocks

At this point I felt that more was needed. Small curved rail blocks between the rail and leg were the choice and these were first sawn to shape and the curve finished on an upturned belt sander (**photo 13**).

Another detail was added—a bevel along the rail edge that was routed with a 45° router cutter and bearing. The small curved blocks also received the same bevel and it was easier to do this before gluing them in place. To do this I clamped some scrap to the bench to cradle the blocks and routed the bevel in with a laminate trimmer. After this, the blocks were glued in place (**photo 14**).

Curved rail supports were sawn and finished on a sander.

The curved detail blocks were glued in place.

After the glue dried I spent some time cleaning up where the blocks meet the rails and then routed in the bevel on the edge of the rails and the remainder of the curved blocks.

Corner blocks are glued and screwed into the table frame at this stage (**photo 15**). These make the frame a lot stronger—I always use them.

The top

Wood was selected for the top and machined up. I layed out the boards and played around with their position to get the best grain arrangement possible. Blackwood can be difficult in this regard as there can be great variation between boards, even when they are from the same tree. Once satisfied with the boards they can be jointed on their edges and glued up.

Another detail

While the top glue was drying I had an objective look at the table design. It seemed that the top and frame were too disparate and needed to be tied together somehow. My solution was to inlay a strip of blackwood down the outsides of the legs. Obviously this would have been easier to accomplish before the frame was assembled. Undeterred, I routed a straight groove down the legs and then fitted and glued in blackwood strips (**photo 16**). This sat proud and was planed down flush when dry (**photo 17**).

Details on top

The top was then sawn to final length and the underneath flattened with a plane and sander. It is fixed to the frame using wood buttons. Next I sanded the top, first with a belt sander moving slightly across the grain to remove material quicker (**photo 18**). After that I sanded with the grain finishing off with a belt sander.

Mitered blocks are glued and screwed into the frame corners to strengthen the frame.

A groove was routed on the outside leg faces.

CUTTING LIST				Measurements in inches/mm
QTY	COMPONENT	LENGTH	WIDTH	THICKNESS
1	top	60 (1520)	35$\frac{1}{2}$ (900)	$\frac{7}{8}$ (21)
1	top inlay strip	15$\frac{3}{4}$ (400)	$\frac{3}{16}$ (4)	$\frac{3}{16}$ (3)
3	top inlay square	1$\frac{1}{2}$ (40)	1$\frac{1}{2}$ (40)	$\frac{3}{16}$ (3)
4	legs	28 (710)	3 (75)	1$\frac{3}{4}$ (45)
4	leg inlay strip	25$\frac{1}{2}$ (650)	$\frac{3}{16}$ (4)	$\frac{3}{16}$ (3)
8	trim for feet	2$\frac{7}{8}$ (72)	3$\frac{1}{4}$ (80)	$\frac{1}{4}$ (6)
8	trim for feet	2 (50)	3$\frac{1}{4}$ (80)	$\frac{1}{4}$ (6)
2	long rails	46$\frac{1}{4}$ (1175)	3$\frac{1}{2}$ (90)	1$\frac{1}{4}$ (32)
2	short rails	30 (760)	3$\frac{1}{2}$ (90)	1$\frac{1}{4}$ (32)
8	curved rail supports	4$\frac{1}{8}$ (105)	1$\frac{1}{2}$ (40)	1$\frac{1}{4}$ (32)
4	mitered corner blocks	6 (150)	2$\frac{3}{8}$ (60)	1$\frac{1}{2}$ (40)

Top inlay

Yet another detail is the inlayed strip and squares in the top. I marked it all out, routed the strip and then the squares with a straight cutter in the laminate trimmer. A chisel cleaned up the edges (**photo 19**) before the strip and then the squares were glued in. This was all flushed down later with a hand plane and sander.

The top edge has the corners rounded and a 15° bevel routed in with a bearing guided router cutter. After that it was time for another final sand and then polishing.

Poly-wax finish

I used a water-based polyurethane which was brushed on. However, as this type of finish is quite white it does not bring out the color of the wood very well. Prior to brushing on the polyurethane I gave the whole table a coat of oil. This highlighted the timber color and was left to dry for three days before the final polish was brushed on. Two coats of polyurethane were applied followed by a gentle sand and a wax-on, wax-off treatment.

Tapping the blackwood strip detail in place.

Sanding first across the grain to remove material quickly.

Chiselling a recess for the inlay on the top.

Tool Box

For site work, maintenance calls, or to repair something in the house, you need something to carry a few tools in. This project gives you a tool box that can hold a basic tool set. It is strong enough to last many years, and if made well, is a small advertisement for the standard of work you are capable of. Only a small amount of timber is needed so choose the best you can afford. In this case I used Brazilian mahogany which was recycled from an old bed-head.

Grain orientation is important to consider for this piece because short grain is the enemy of wood strength. Imagine a square of wood—if you sawed $\frac{1}{2}$" (12mm) off the long grain side that strip would be flexible enough to bend without easily breaking. If however you sawed $\frac{1}{2}$" off the end of the square, that piece would be very weak because it is all short grain.

With this tool box there is potential for weakness because normally when you make a box, the grain on the sides and ends would be arranged to run the same way (horizontal). If you do this here though, there will be a section of short grain supporting the handle which will probably break in time.

The solution then is to run the end sections with the grain vertical in order to give long grain support to the handle. The compromise is that the dovetail joint at the box corner has long and short grain meeting. If the pins are too fine on the end pieces there will be weak short grain so keep these pins large to maintain strength. It's also not advisable to make the sides too wide, up to $5\frac{1}{2}$" (140mm) is okay.

1 The first process is to plane and thickness the wood to the desired measurements, as well as to cut all pieces to length. The working measurements for this box are 17¾" (450mm) long, 7" (180mm) wide and the end pieces are 10" (250mm) long. Naturally you can alter these dimensions to suit. The handle is 1" (26mm) square and 17" (430mm) long.

2

Mark out all the dovetails on the side pieces. Ensure the pins at the ends are a reasonable size to avoid short grain weakness. In practice, the pin on the corner wil be supported by the base which will add strength. I used a knife to mark the tails.

3

Saw the tails, working to the knife line. If you're not experienced at hand cutting dovetails consider using a jig. It is vital that the saw kerf lines up with the knife mark to ensure a tight fit.

4

With the tails cut, the side is layed over the end piece and the pins are marked. Check with a square that both pieces are at 90° to each other before placing the marks. Again a knife is used for marking.

5

The shoulders have to be levelled and you can do this with a sharp chisel. By making a few saw cuts first most of the waste can be removed and the chisel will clean up what remains.

6

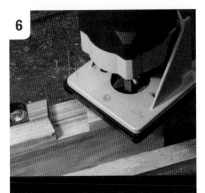

Another option is to use a router cutter in a laminate trimmer to remove the waste and leave the shoulders square and clean.

7

Test fit the joint at this stage. It is a good idea to relieve the inside edge of the tails. Do this with a chisel.

8

The handle is made from square sectioned wood which is later shaped. Its position is marked on the endpieces and most of the waste removed with a Forstner bit in the drill press.

9

The hole now needs to be made square. Mark the corners and clean up with a chisel so that the handle material is a neat fit in the square hole.

10

The end pieces are shaped by sawing the corners off at an angle. Use a bandsaw or jigsaw to remove the waste. I actually went a bit further here and put in a curve before the straight line, this is more work but adds some extra detail.

11

Use a handplane to clean up the edge.

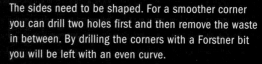

The sides need to be shaped. For a smoother corner you can drill two holes first and then remove the waste in between. By drilling the corners with a Forstner bit you will be left with an even curve.

12

HANDMADE FURNITURE

13

The sides need to cleaned up with a plane and sandpaper.

14

The handle edges are relieved by using a 45° chamfer bit mounted in the laminate trimmer. Take two or three passes to reach the desired depth.

15

Prior to gluing up, the inside faces need to be sanded and detailed as much as possible. Only sand lightly the inside corners, remove too much and the joint will have a gap. Once you are satisfied with the components the box can be glued together and set aside to dry.

CUTTING LIST   *Measurements in inches/mm*

QTY	COMPONENT	LENGTH	WIDTH	THICKNESS
2	sides	17³/₄ (450)	4³/₄ (120)	¹/₂ (11)
2	ends	10 (250)	7 (180)	³/₄ (19)
1	base	17³/₄ (450)	7 (180)	¹/₂ (11)
1	handle	17 (430)	1 (26)	1 (26)

Finishing off

Remove any glue runs and sand the box again. Plane the lower edges level to accept the base. You can use solid timber for the base because there is no conflict in grain direction. I used ³/₈" (10mm) thick timber; this is glued on but needs the extra support of screws at the ends. Countersink six gauge screws ³/₄" (19mm) long. Shellac is a good choice for the polish, apply this and finish off with a buffed wax.

The chest is a traditional piece of furniture with a long history of making and usage. This one has a basic box construction with an inner drawer.

Blanket Box

The modern incarnation of the chest is the 'blanket box' and if this doubles as a seat it needs to be strong enough to support weight as well. This project is no more than a box with lid and base. Dowels are the primary jointing method throughout and the top and base use a floating panel within a frame. A small sliding drawer resides within and is also dowelled together.

Selecting and matching

Select the timber for the main box and try and match up grain and color as best as possible. Blackwood is a difficult wood to grain match as there is so much variation within each board. Where possible, I used the same board for each panel. The front is made from one wide board cut in half and then glued up with the grain running in the same direction.

QTY	COMPONENT	LENGTH	WIDTH	THICKNESS
2	sides	15³/₈ (390)	16¹/₈ (410)	³/₄ (20)
2		30³/₄ (780)	16¹/₈ (410)	³/₄ (20)
2	top frame	35¹/₂ (900)	2³/₈ (60)	³/₄ (20)
2		13³/₄ (350)	2³/₄ (70)	³/₄ (20)
2	base frame	33¹/₂ (854)	2¹/₄ (60)	³/₄ (20)
2		13³/₄ (350)	2 (50)	³/₄ (20)
2	panels	30¹/₂ (772)	14¹/₄ (362)	³/₄ (18)
2	drawer sides	17³/₄ (450)	3¹/₂ (90)	¹/₂ (12)
2		14³/₈ (365)	3¹/₂ (90)	¹/₂ (12)
2	ply base approx.	17¹/₈ (434)	14⁵/₈ (372)	³/₁₆ (4)

CUTTING LIST *Measurements in inches/mm*

Scale: 1:10

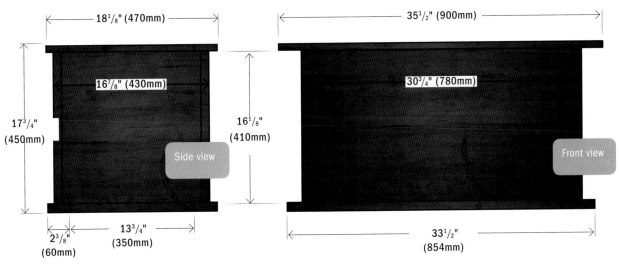

18¹/₈" (470mm)

16⁷/₈" (430mm)

17³/₄" (450mm)

13³/₄" (350mm)

2³/₈" (60mm)

Side view

35¹/₂" (900mm)

30³/₄" (780mm)

16¹/₈" (410mm)

33¹/₂" (854mm)

Front view

The dowel locations are marked out on the end grain of the side panels. Here I used ³/₈" (10mm) diameter dowels that were 2" (50mm) long.

Glue up the four box panels and then dimension these to size. I plane one edge, saw it to width with the planed edge against the saw fence, and then plane the freshly sawn edge. The panel is then sawn to length.

The dowel positions are transferred to the mating panel. I used a drill press to drill the panel, however you could use a dowel jig for this. Chamfering the dowel holes with a countersinking drill bit made inserting the dowels easier.

Use a jig to drill the holes in the end grain. I drilled deep enough for the dowels to protrude around ¹/₂" (15mm) as this is the amount of dowel that goes into the holes in the long panels. The masking tape on the drill bit was my depth stop.

Now is the time to sand the inside faces of the panels—the outside is easy to sand later. Glue and tap the dowels into the short panels.

I used three clamps on each joint with sticks to spread the pressure. Make sure the box is square and none of the sides are bowed. I placed some spacers inside to keep everything parallel.

Do a dry test fit to ensure everything aligns and if okay apply glue to the joint and tap everything home.

Making the frames and panels

There are a few ways you can make a lid. A single solid panel could do the trick but it would need something to keep it flat. Breadboard ends are an option—here mortise and tenon joints, and a tongue and groove locate the breadboard end with the panel. Another option is a solid panel with cleats underneath that allow wood movement.

The lid and base on my box, however, are a frame and panel construction. The frame keeps everything flat whilst 'floating' the panel accommodates wood movement. Strength is covered by using $^{11}/_{16}$" (18mm) thick blackwood.

The frames use three dowels. Drill the holes for these first.

The panel sits within a groove in the frame made with a straight cutter in the router table. The groove is $^{3}/_{8}$" (10mm) wide and $^{1}/_{4}$" (8mm) deep (the size of the cutter in the router table) and runs the length of the short pieces but is stopped on the longer pieces.

The top and base panels are $^{3}/_{4}$" (18mm) thick and have a tongue machined in all edges. The final size of the panel depends on the depth of the groove in the frame and the size of the tongue. I used a $^{1}/_{2}$" (12mm) rebating cutter on the panel and made the tongue to be a neat fit in the groove. This fit will be determined to an extent by the weather conditions at assembly time. For instance in very wet weather wood will swell giving a firmer fit.

Gluing up the lid and base

Sand the panels before gluing the whole frame assembly. It's important to center the panels with an even gap all around. Measuring and making line-up marks on the panel and short pieces will ensure this. The panels need to be without twist when they are glued. The ouside of the main box can be sanded now. The top and lower frame are also final sanded. I use a belt sander and plane to flatten the frame. There will be some variation in alignment at the joint line.

The base is now glued and screwed to the main box.

Inner drawer

The drawer was made from Huon pine and fits neatly within the sides. Once the box was made I measured for the drawer and left a $^1/_{16}$" (1mm) clearance so that the drawer was 18$^7/_8$" (480mm) long x 15$^3/_8$" (389mm) wide overall. The sides are 3$^1/_2$" (90mm) high and $^1/_2$" (12mm) thick. A black-wood veneered plywood panel sits in grooves which were sawn into the sides.

My drawer is dowelled together but you can use through dovetails at the corners if want a more decorative touch.

The drawer slides from end to end on two $^3/_4$" x $^3/_4$" (20mm x 20mm) cleats of blackwood which are screwed along the sides about 4$^3/_4$" (120mm) down from the top edge of the box.

Fitting the lid

Two hinges are used to attach the lid to the box. Fit the hinge in the box first by laying it in position and using a knife to outline it. A small cutter in a laminate trimmer will remove most of the waste. The depth of routing is equal to just under half of the thickness of the hinge knuckle. Insert the hinges and fit the screws neatly. Expect variations in individual hinge manufacture and mark each hinge on the inside so that it always returns to its same position. The top was then laid in position and a knife used to mark the hinge positions. I couldn't trace the hinges with the top in the way so each hinge was removed and laid in place on the top to get the location right. Once again the laminate trimmer removed most of the waste with a chisel cleaning up. The hinge can be dropped in place and the holes drilled.

A small chain is fitted inside to prevent the top leaning back too far and ripping the hinges out.

Finishing off

To soften all the sharp edges I ran the laminate trimmer with a small rounding over bit along all the top and base edges. The outside edge of the box was relieved with a small stopped chamfer.

The finish chosen was an oil and wax combination. Two coats of oil were liberally applied a few days apart. Then the box was given two coats of wax and buffed.

This box is a simple construction which can be varied by using exposed corner joints or by adding any number of details. As storage, seat or a table surface, the chest is a multi-function furniture item that's sure to find a purpose in the average home.

Mitered and Keyed Boxes

Fine work and tolerances make

boxmaking an intense but

effective way to hone your skills.

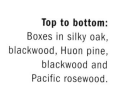

Top to bottom:
Boxes in silky oak,
blackwood, Huon pine,
blackwood and
Pacific rosewood.

Respect. That's what I have for boxmakers. With cabinetmaking there is always a small margin allowed for adjusting the fit of components. Doors can be be planed half a millimetre or so to allow for an even gap, and likewise drawers can be coaxed to an even fit. But when you make a box the whole scale of work is reduced and so therefore is the margin. This is detail work that requires good eyesight and a commitment to perfection.

The size you make a box will be determined by its intended function, or by the materials you wish to use. Selecting and matching solid and veneered wood is always important but especially so on small scale work. Box lids, both inner and outer, are perfect for displaying highly figured wood, but remember that visually speaking less can sometimes be more. Lid frames and box sides can be made of similar or contrasting species. Give some thought to how the grain will flow around lid frames and sides and choose the best arrangement.

If making a box to house certain items, take the time to accurately calculate the internal measurements and any partitions, trays or compartments which may be needed. In a sense you will need to calculate from the inside out to arrive at your external dimensions.

Before you start give consideration to how the box will be opened—will you incorporate a fingerpull, a groove or a catch? Will you use a chain or a stay to prevent the lid falling back? Will you fit magnets, a lock or a catch, or none of these to keep the lid closed?

Batches

Whether your box design is straightforward or elaborate, as with most woodwork, once things are set up and you get going, it is just as easy to make more than one of the same item. The five boxes shown were made as a batch even though they were made from different species—blackwood, silky oak, Huon pine and Pacific rosewood.

The boxes shown here are $9^1/_2$ x $5^1/_2$ x $3^1/_8$" (240 x 140 x 80mm) deep. The Huon box is slightly smaller because I happened to notice a split in one piece of wood and had to cut it out late in the making, thus reducing the size. One box was made to store router cutters and needed to be 4" (100mm) deep (see p.76). For the lid infills I selected the best veneers I had.

The corners and lid of each box are mitered and have keys to reinforce them. The keys are small pieces of timber with the grain running across the miter so they offer some long grain surface area for a greater bond. Using keys in contrasting timber creates an interesting design feature that you can experiment with.

I prepared all the timber in one batch. The box sides were machined to $3/_8$" (10mm) thickness but the lid pieces were taken to $7/_{16}$" (11mm). The lid is thicker because you need a little extra meat to work with when machining in grooves and slots. Extra wood was machined up to allow for timber defects and any mistakes on my behalf. I like to work with lengths that are as long as possible—they're much safer to machine.

The lid infills also need to be prepared. My boxes have veneered panels—thin veneer leaves were glued to

both sides of a ⅛" (3mm) MDF core. The groove for the plywood lid infill was sawn on the tablesaw before any miters were cut (**photo 1**).

Miters

The base of the boxes are veneered ply panels. These are ⅛" thick and sit in a corresponding groove in the side. These grooves were also sawn on the tablesaw.

The miters on the sides and lid were sawn with the power miter saw. Stops were clamped to the metal fence to allow repeat cuts. It's much easier to fine sand the inside of the sides before sizing them to length and before assembling. The outsides are easy to sand later.

Cut all the long sides and the long lid lengths then the short sides and lid pieces. With the shorter lengths

I press them against the fence with a piece of wood about 12" (300mm) long so that my fingers are well clear of the blade. Never compromise your fingers for the sake of a little piece of wood. Use some of the extra lengths you machined to saw some test miters to make sure the saw is cutting accurately; basically the miters need to be perfect (**photo 2**). With modern machinery it is pretty well possible to have a perfect miter; the problems arise when we revert back to our hands to assemble it.

Assembly

With the side miters sawn the box can be assembled. Take one short and one long side and apply glue to the end grain on both pieces, then bring the miter together.

Place the base in now and wrap the sides around. Using good quality masking tape, stretch the tape over the joint. Work quickly but carefully. The masking tape exerts an amazing amount of pressure, the only possible problem is that the tape can tear out some fibres on softer woods. Repeat the procedure with the other long and short sides then bring the two halves together, using tape again to hold the joint together (**photo 3**). Check it for square.

I then used an appropriately named miter belt clamp to hold the box together (**photo 4**). Make any adjustments to bring it into square then set it aside to dry.

When dry, saw in the slots for the keys. For this I used a biscuit joiner. The box was clamped to the bench top and the joiner fence held against the top edges of the box. Carefully but with firm control of the tool the jointer was plunged into the wood. It is critical that the power tool approaches the miter at exactly 90° so that the slot is evenly positioned with equal extension on each box side. I made marks on the joiner fence to align it (**photos 5, 6**). You can also make a 'cradle' and cut these slots on the tablesaw as I did for my wall boxes (see p.79).

The slot formed is about ¹/₈" (mm) wide (depending on the type of saw fitted to the biscuit joiner) and extends in this case ⁹/₁₆" (15mm) along the sides. I placed two keys along each miter except for the heavier router cutter box which has four keys.

Keys

The keys are made from strips of wood machined to be a neat fit in the slots. Before gluing the keys into the slots I hammered the keys a little to compress the wood slightly to enable them to slip easily into the slots. When the wood absorbs the glue it swells up locking the joint (**photo 7**).

When the glue is dry the keys can be sawn flush with the sides of the box. Be careful not to chip out the short grain at the corner. It is therefore better to saw towards the box (**photo 8**).

Lids

The lids can now be assembled. The veneered plywood infill should be a snug fit in the groove (**photo 9**).

A small amount of glue is applied to secure the infill in place and a more generous amount applied at the

miters. Once again masking tape is securely stretched over the miter to hold it in place. I then secured the lid with some small clamps until the glue set. With the lid dry, slots now need to be cut in the miter for keys to be placed. Once again I use the biscuit joiner to cut the slots. It is worth sawing quite a few test pieces to ensure the slot is positioned centrally in the thickness of the wood. Keys are then glued in place (**photo 10**).

Because everything was sawn at the same time the lid should be a perfect fit on the box sides. The lid does need to be cleaned up and flattened before it is fitted to the box. I used a combination of block plane and sanding block to level the lid miters. There is no real short cut here to produce a neat even fitting lid other than careful planing and sanding.

Quality brass hinges were used. To install these a small straight bit was fitted into a laminate trimmer to rout the housing for the hinge flaps. To avoid problems drilling the holes for the screws I use a self centring drill bit to position the bit in the center of the brass hole and thus prevent the screw wandering off-center. Once I was satisfied with the fit of the hinges the boxes were given their first sand on the outside. I inverted my belt sander on the bench and sanded the lid and box side flush.

Fitting magnets as catches

Magnets were used to act as catches but another option is to purchase brass catches that fit to the outside of the box. The magnets I used are $^3/_{16}$" (4mm) in diameter. Mark the position where the magnet will go in the box side and then tap a small brad into the wood. Snip the head of the brad off to leave around $^3/_{32}$" (2mm) protruding and then close the lid—this will mark the lid where the opposing magnet needs to be. Remove the brad and drill matching holes for the magnets. Drill and experiment on scrap wood to find the drill bit size and depth to house the magnet. The magnets I used needed a slightly smaller drill hole. Glue in one magnet with superglue and tap it level with the wood (any minor protrusion of the magnet can be sanded flush later), then glue in the opposing magnet. Take care that the magnets are oriented correctly so that they do not repel each other.

The recess which acts as a finger pull was routed in with a 45° chamfer bit in a laminate trimmer. The box can now be fine sanded and prepared for polishing. In this case two coats of shellac were applied followed by two coats of oil. Everything was sanded between coats and then buffed to finish off.

Router cutter box

Router cutters are a significant investment so they are worth protecting. Keeping them dust free is important, as is ensuring they don't knock against each other. Safely housed, your cutters will stay sharper longer.

Unlike the boxes shown at the start of this project, this box was 4" (100mm) deep (excluding the lid).

The router cutter box has a solid wood insert 1$^1/_4$" (32mm) thick which could also be made from thick plywood. The insert sits inside the box flush with the base.

Holes were drilled in the insert slightly over $^1/_4$" and $^1/_2$" in diameter to accept standard sized cutter shanks. The holes were drilled deeply (but not all the way through) to house the cutters.

Wall Boxes

A vertical storage and

display solution.

Boxes. What interesting and fun things they are to make. But what if you could use a box in other ways? How about if you put it on the wall? Then you could put your keys in it, or your medicine, your artifacts...or whatever. So that's how my wall boxes came about. In fact, if you google 'wall boxes' you will find that heaps of other people have had the same bright idea. We could ask the question: at what point does a box become a cabinet? But cabinets can be free-standing or non-fixed so we'll leave that debate for another time.

These boxes are made using King Billy pine from Tasmania and Douglas fir from Canada, both selected because they are amongst my favourite timbers. And they are lightweight, a benefit for a piece that will hang on a wall.

Designing your box

Before you begin you need to sort the measurements out. For these boxes I played around with the dimensions by moving pieces of wood around on my benchtop till the proportions were to my liking. From this process, and by also looking more closely at other boxes, I found what I feel is a good balance between length and width. These particular wall boxes are 7¼" (185mm) wide and 20" (510mm) high. However you may prefer a different proportion, perhaps wider or even longer.

The making

As is usual for me, I standardised wood dimensions for both the boxes shown: in this case ⁵/₈" (16mm) thick and 3³/₄" (95mm) wide. That means I can run all the wood through the machines at one setting and save time. The wood was first squared up and the pieces left slightly oversize in length for final trimming later.

These boxes have a plywood back, but you could also use a thin solid wood panel. At this stage I sawed in a groove for the plywood using the tablesaw. This is a quick and accurate way to make grooves. Just check that the width of the groove is a good fit with the plywood you are using (**photo 1**).

Joints

Miters are used for the side joints. Personally I find miters a rather slow joint to make if you cut them on the tablesaw. If you use the tablesaw you have to fiddle around with the blade tilt and adjust the sliding table. The miter (or drop) saw is my machine of choice for this joint, depending on how wide the material is. As these boxes are only 3³/₄" (95mm) wide I was able to use the drop saw to cut the miter. What I do find with the miter saw though is that sharpness is very important.

Pre-assembly

After the miters are cut, check they are correct and then fine sand or plane the insides of the boxes. Make sure the plywood is sized correctly and don't be afraid to do a dry assembly of all the pieces.

Assembly

Lay all the pieces inside-down and end-to-end, push masking tape onto the miters, then flip the lot over. Now apply glue to the end grain—I put glue on both ends of each joint. Drop in the plywood back and start folding the box together (**photos 2, 3, 4**). Now put on more masking

Making a miter sled

A With the components sawn to length glue one half of the sled together.

B The other half can be glued on, but take care to keep things parallel.

C Use screws to strengthen the sled, but make sure the screws don't foul the sawblade

D The 'mouth' of the sled will need to be carefully opened up with a chisel.

WALL BOXES

79

Wall boxes in celery top pine with blackheart sassafras panels.

that gives a flat bottomed kerf. A rip blade with flat top teeth is the blade of choice for this.

For the sled I prepared small pieces of wood that were able to accept $3^{25}/_{32}$" (96mm). This leaves a $^3/_{64}$" (1mm) clearance for the $3^3/_4$" (95mm) wide boxes. Screws reinforce the glue joints. The mouth of the sled may need to be tuned with a chisel.

The sled with a box mounted in it can be easily slid over the spinning sawblade. The spacing of the saw cuts is adjusted by moving the saw fence. Be careful when sawing because the miters are only held by glue at this stage and won't handle any rough shocks (**photo 5**).

Miter keys

These little miter keys are fiddly to make but are an important part of the box. I used the same wood for the keys but you can use a contrasting color for an excellent effect. Glue the keys in and when dry saw them flush and trim with a plane or chisel (**photo 6**).

If hand sawing the keys flush, be careful to cut towards the box or you can push part of the key out at the corner and then you will have to glue the torn wood back in.

Shelves

Next I made and fitted the shelves. The shelves are the same thickness as the other box components but are only 3" (75mm) wide. I set these back $^3/_{16}$" (5mm) from the front edge. The shelves are held in position with bamboo 'dowels'. These are actually bought as barbeque skewers at the supermarket.

A $^5/_{32}$" (4mm) hole provides an almost perfect fit for a piece of bamboo skewer. I apply glue to the shelves and push them in place ensuring they are square and then leave to dry. With the drill press I drill the $^5/_{32}$" holes and glue in the bamboo dowels. The ends of the bamboo can be sawn and sanded flush.

tape, but really apply pressure. The simple taping process does a good job of clamping. However I often still use light clamps if the miter does not come together perfectly with the masking tape alone. Check the box is square and leave it to dry overnight.

Miter sled

Small wood keys are used to strengthen the miter joint. The best way to cut the slot for the keys is with a miter sled. This supports the box as it is passed over the table-saw blade. Small pieces of wood (keys) are then glued in the slots. It is important to use a sawblade

Doors

The door components are $1^1/_2 x^5/_8$" (40x16mm).
Rather than have short rails, I made them extend
to the end so the stile butts onto them. I used a $^1/_4$"
(6mm) thick solid wood panel that sits in a sawed-in
groove. By using the tablesaw to make the groove I
traded speed for a resulting groove visible on the rail
ends. These grooves need to be plugged with small
pieces of wood. I used the same wood for this but
again you could use a contrasting color (**photo 7**).

The hinges are housed in flush and for this I used
my laminate trimmer with a small cutter. By using
the trimmer fence as a depth stop the housing can
be made with a flat base and a clean line (**photo 8**).
The corners will still need to be squared with a chisel
(**photo 9**). Each hinge is individually fitted—you can't
assume hinges are equal.

I like the look of square-drive screws. A self-centering drill guide and bit are used to drill holes exactly in the centers of the hinge holes for the screws (**photo 10**). The catches for the doors are small magnets glued into matching holes in the door and box edge.

For the handles I used small pieces of wood ⅞ x ¼" (22 x 5mm) that are fitted in small mortises. The edges were relieved slightly to be gentle on the fingers.

Mounting

Wall boxes need some form of mounting system. The system I used is called a French cleat and is made up of two pieces of wood that mate at an angle. You can rip a piece of wood at about 30° to give you the pieces you need. One piece is fixed to the back of the box and the other is mounted on the wall (**photo 11**). The latter piece must be level. The box with the attached cleat is lifted onto the wall-mounted cleat and will just sit in place held by gravity and friction.

Polishing

After all the making processes it is inevitable that there will be a few small bumps and marks on the boxes. Sanding is usually enough to get everything smooth and pristine, however deeper marks may need to be ironed out. A damp cloth held over the offending dent with a hot iron applied to it will steam out most marks.

A coat of clear oil was first applied to the boxes followed by two coats of water-based lacquer. You can of course use the finish of your choice.

Router Bit Box

A cutaway and a 'fold-over' lid

make a handy storage box.

Some years ago I made myself the small box shown on p.76 to hold router cutters. Small was the operative word, because at some point it was no longer big enough. The cutters had to be crammed in and were hard to extract. There ended up being about 10 cutters without designated positions that were just thrown in randomly. Rather than protecting my valuable cutters the box became a liability. On the outside it still looked good but it didn't function well. Time for a better storage box.

Design and planning

The plan was to make a box that had a thick base with holes drilled for the router cutters. The front of the box is cutaway for easier access to the bits. The lid needs to compensate for the cutaway and my solution was to have a lid with an attached face that acts as a 'fold'. The fold covers the cutaway area to keep the box as dustproof as possible.

Base layout

Count how many cutters you have now (give away the ones you never use—and be realistic for example

with, say, dovetail bits that are worn and blunt) but leave room for future purchases. The overall box dimensions will be dictated by this to a large extent. However I wanted the box to be as sleek as possible so I figured out a minimum height that would still house everything.

I used Forstner bits to drill half and quarter inch diameter holes into the base to hold the cutters. I made the holes 1" (25mm) deep, deeming this a good size to comfortably hold the cutters. The base is $1^{1}/_{4}$" (30mm) thick so there is $^{1}/_{4}$" (5mm) of solid wood below the end of the cutter shank in the base for strength. To be honest MDF or plywood would be better for the base, as these materials have virtually no movement in width. However, we are talking woodwork here.

I used a piece of quartersawn Huon pine as the base and only spot glued it on one long edge when fitting it inside the box. As the base is not very wide any wood movement should be minimal.

In a test piece of wood I trialled the fit and position of both large and small cutters and decided on a final arrangement of the hole positions. I worked out how

A blackwood box customised to hold router bits that features a 'fold-over' lid with a 'live' or waney edge.

high the longest cutters would protrude from the base and found the overall height of the box sides would need to be $3^3/_8$" (85mm) (**photo 1**). The lid will add extra height.

There are three rows of holes. The $^1/_4$" holes are at the back and there are two rows with $^1/_2$" holes staggered to give large cutters clearance from each other. The final dimension for the base was $15^3/_4$" (400mm) long and $4^3/_8$" (110mm) wide (**photos 2, 3**). The base can be made a little longer and wider so it can be custom fitted inside the box later. The main thing is to plan the sequence of making as best you can and hope you don't forget any processes.

Box carcase construction

The box sides are $3^3/_8$" (85mm) high and mitered at the corners. Keys are added to the miter for strength. Miters are not critical—you could butt join the sides with dowels, or go for it and dovetail the thing together. You could nail and glue it too but that's not the point here.

Before the box sides are assembled a cutaway has to be formed in the front long side. Mark the cutaway in pencil and locate the corners. Drill the corners in the cutaway with a Forstner bit to give a neat smooth curve (**photo 4**). I decided on a slight angle for the cutaway sides (**photo 5**).

A bandsaw or jigsaw can be used to complete the

cutaway (**photo 6**). Use a plane to clean up the sawn edges. You can follow up with a chisel, and then use sandpaper wrapped around a piece of wood to help ensure straight and flat sanding (**photos 7**).

Box assembly

Sand the inside faces and glue the box sides together. As this is a small piece, stretching masking tape across the miters supplies a surprising amount of pressure. Normally with small boxes this will be enough to close the miters up. Check all is square and set aside to dry overnight.

The 'folding' lid

The overall dimensions of the lid are $15^3/_4$x$4^{15}/_{16}$" (400 x 126mm). As you can see I used sapwood or a 'live' edge for this 'folding' piece of wood but a sawn square edged piece would also be fine.

My first lid (yes, first) was from solid quartersawn wood. My figuring was that dry stable wood only $4^{15}/_{16}$" wide would be cool regarding movement and any associated problems. After dimensioning the lid and beautifully fitting it to the sides with brass hinges it twisted. Next...

Plywood core with veneer faces was the material chosen for the second lid. The live edge would still happen but the veneered ply would avoid most wood movement. Plywood $^1/_2$" (12mm) thick was selected and dimensioned oversize then veneer glued to both faces using cauls and clamps (**photo 8**). After drying,

the panel was sawn to final dimensions. This allowed for the solid wood lippings applied to the rear and side edges. I made the lid oversize in width though, so the front edge could be lined up after the hinges were fitted. I glued the end lippings first and then the rear one. These lippings are about $^{1}/_{64}$" (0.5mm) thicker than the veneered lid panel (**photo 9**). After the lippings had dried they were flushed with the veneer. You can sand, plane or scrape them level with the veneer. Be careful here not to break through the veneer.

Fitting the lid

Small brass hinges are used but take care with screw length, you don't want to have a screw point coming out of the face of the lid. The lid will need to be $^{1}/_{2}$" (13mm) or more, thick to offer enough purchase for

wood screws to bite into. I used $^{1}/_{2}$" long square-drive screws. These needed to be shortened with pliers.

With the lid hinged I could mark where the front edge needed to be sawn, then plane it in preparation to receive the folding live edge. When I was happy with the fit of everything the folding piece of wood was glued onto the lid and left to dry (**photos 10, 11**).

All that is now left to do is the final detailing. This includes sanding everything flush and cleaning up any dents or scratches (**photo 12**). Small dents can be removed with steam: place a damp cloth over the surface and run a hot iron over the top. Get a feel for this method on scrap wood first. The dented or compacted wood fibres will swell up when steam is applied. The box was finished with shellac and wax.

A Simple Cabinet

A small blackwood cabinet

which is easy to make.

Dowels are the principal method of joinery for this small cabinet. It's a different sort of construction for me because normally I would use a frame and panel method for the sides and then fix the top with buttons to allow for wood movement.

In this case however, the sides are solid panels glued to the legs and the top and base are also glued in place. The grain orientation of the sides, base and top follow in the same direction hence there is no conflict in allowing for timber movement. I made the cabinet by cutting the components, marking dowel positions, drilling dowel holes, sanding, assembling and finally polishing it.

Dowels are fairly simple to use, a dowelling drill bit and jig are the only specialised equipment you will need with the possible addition of a drill press. Dowels are available milled and cut to length and various standard industry sizes are available. For this cabinet 3/8" (9.5mm) diameter dowels 2" (50mm) long were used. Australian blackwood was my choice of wood for this cabinet. To add a bit of contrast I used Huon pine veneered over plywood for the door panels.

Machine all the wood at the same time. The legs are squared up, panels are planed and thicknessed, then everything is sawn to length. The sides and base are all the same width, although you will later need to add trim pieces to the base to increase its width to fill the gaps. When sawing always keep offcuts handy. These become test pieces for setting up the dowelling jig or the position of the grooves in the rails.

There are three rails for the cabinet, the front one is fixed horizontally while the two rear ones are fixed vertically. The base panel sits flush with the sides and the top is dowelled into the top of the side panels. While the door is drying the top can be glued in place. If you are going to do any edge moulding to the top it's better to do this before gluing it in place. In this case I ran a rounding over bit along the top edge and then a small 45° bevel bit on the lower edge. Inside the cabinet are two gaps on either edge of the base panel. I made a Huon pine slip to fit in the rear gap and a blackwood slip to glue on the from edge. The door needs to be finished now. A small blackwood strip was glued over the center of the door panel. This was purely for appearance and is optional.

Plane and sand the door rails flush and fit the door to the opening. Quality brass hinges should be used to hang the door. I used a pair of magnets to act as a door catch. One was housed in a small triangular piece of wood fitted inside the cabinet where the top inner corner of the door would touch against it. The other magnet was fitted into the door to make contact.

A small brass knob was fitted centrally on the door. The internal shelf is 1/2" (12mm) thick and sits on the pre-drilled brass sleeves. The cabinet back now needs to be fitted—the one on this cabinet was made of solid Huon pine 3 9/16" wide x 3/8" (90x 10mm). The Huon was ship-lapped on the edges with a rebating router cutter. The boards were screwed into the rear rails. The cabinet was fine sanded and then oiled.

1

Use a dowelling jig to guide the drill bit. The narrow rails are being drilled here. The piece of masking tape on the drill bit is the depth stop. These dowel holes can also be drilled on a mortising table.

2

The holes are neatly drilled. Before you get started spend some time drilling offcuts until you are satisfied with the centering of the holes and then drill the components.

The position of the dowels must be marked before drilling the legs. I use a fine ink pen to mark the wood and then an awl to mark the exact center of the hole.

If your dowelling jig can't be used on thicker wood then the holes can be drilled on the drill press. The legs are being drilled here to accept the vertical rear rails.

On the panels, the dowels need to be marked on the edges. Mark one panel and then use this as a reference guide. Clamp this to the other panels to be sure of exact matching positions.

The edges of the panel after drilling.

The holes in the panels must match the holes in the legs. Here the panel is brought up to the legs and the positions transferred. Note the ink marks on the top of the leg, these are to make sure the legs aren't mixed up.

The holes in the legs are drilled for the panels—once again on the drill press. Note the piece of wood clamped to the drill press table—this acts as a fence for drilling multiple holes at the same distance from the edge.

9

Apply glue to the dowels and tap them into the panels. Once the dowels are inserted the panels are ready to be glued to the legs. One thing more though—the cabinet has a center shelf that sits on brass sleeves. The holes for the sleeves should be drilled now before assembly takes place.

10

With all the holes drilled everything is sanded before assembly. Dowel alignment is checked to make sure it will all go together as planned. Now is the time to take the router to the legs and ease the outside edges. I used a small rounding over bit for this.

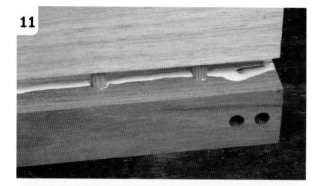

11

Apply glue along the leg and run some into the dowel holes, then bring the pieces together and clamp. You need just the right amount of glue to secure the joint but you don't want glue pouring out and making a huge mess.

12

The side panels were glued to the legs first. Note that clamps are applied top and bottom to give an even spread of pressure. Using clamps like this helps to eliminate any cupping during the glue-up.

13

The dowel holes in the sides for accepting the base could only be drilled to around $1/2$" (15mm) depth. The dowels therefore needed to be trimmed in length before assembly.

14

The base panel was glued to the sides. This was checked for fit before applying glue—you may need to plane a whisker off the sides to fit the base between the legs. When satisfied it can be glued in.

15

The rails and base are glued up and the cabinet checked for square and any twist. The aluminium clamps are great because on a small cabinet like this their light weight won't throw a twist into the cabinet.

16

CUTTING LIST			Measurements in inches/mm
QTY COMPONENT	LENGTH	WIDTH	THICKNESS
4 legs	27¹/₂ (700)	1⁵/₈ (42)	1⁵/₈ (42)
2 side panels	17³/₄ (450)	10¹/₂ (265)	³/₄ (19)
1 base	14 (355)	10¹/₂ (265)	³/₄ (19)
1 top	19¹/₈ (485)	14¹/₂ (370)	³/₄ (19)
1 shelf	14 (353)	10¹/₄ (260)	¹/₂ (12)
3 rails	13 (330)	1¹/₂ (40)	³/₄ (19)
2 door	16¹/₈ (423)	1³/₄ (45)	³/₄ (19)
	9³/₈ (238)	1³/₄ (45)	³/₄ (19)
1 door panel	13³/₄ (350)	9³/₄ (250)	³/₁₆ (4.2)

Note the small pieces of wood used under the clamp heads. These spread pressure and also direct it where needed.

The dowel holes were drilled first in the door rails. The panel was prepared by veneering both sides of some plywood which was cut oversize by about $^3/_4$" (20mm) on all sides. Huon pine veneer $^1/_{32}$" (0.6mm) was pressed onto the plywood. When cured the veneered plywood was measured for thickness. A groove that matched the veneered plywood thickness was sawn into the rails on the tablesaw. The panel can now be sawn to final dimension and the door glued up.

The back of the cabinet showing ship lapped Huon pine boards screwed to the carcase.

Inside the cabinet a small fillet of Huon pine was glued in place to fill the gap between the base and the rear lower rail.

A triangle of blackwood was glued and fixed into the top left corner to house one of the magnets. A matching magnet was fitted into the door rail to act as a catch.

Storage Tower

A cabinet for storing the
ever-changing shape of
digital storage devices.

M ost woodworkers have as many lives as cats. Believe it or not, in my early twenties I went for a short time by the title of 'senior computer operator'. In those days a single computer filled an entire room, and my duty was to keep some very large disks spinning. Some how my 'seniority' meant mainly doing the night shift, but a small stowed-away mattress helped the time pass a bit quicker.

Thankfully computers are a lot smaller now but there seems to be a never-ending succession of digital hardware and back up storage devices. From floppies to zips, to CDs, DVDs, BluRays and all manner of portable hard drives there's no telling where things are headed, meaning that building a unit to store them needs to be adaptable. The cabinet shown here is a development of some CD towers I made some years ago and was designed to house the DVDs that nowadays still form part of the average 'home entertainment system'. You can of course customise the shelf heights to store other things, or if you're reading this story quite a while after it was published you can customise it to whatever the newest kind of digital media is.

The CD tower has an open shelf system that uses mitered corners and a matching 45° chunky solid base. This project is based on the CD tower but holds DVD sized disks, incorporates a door and has the improvement of a constructed base. The starting point for this tower is therefore the base measurement of the DVD case. I set the inside width $^3/_8$" (10mm) larger than the size of a DVD case, $7^{11}/_{16}$" (195mm) and $5^3/_4$" (145mm) deep. The height is arbitrary, I set it at $35^1/_2$" (900mm) with three shelves.

Wood and grain

The timber used here is Queensland white cedar (*Melia azedarach*) a deciduous Australian native species that is reputed to have flowers that smell like chocolate, but fruit that is poisonous to humans. White cedar shares some of the working properties of red cedar but is less durable. I've used this wood a couple of times now and found it relatively easy to plane and chisel. Like red cedar it has pronounced grain markings which can look good if used the right way.

One of the most important things about making furniture from wood is planning the arrangement of the wood grain in the various components. The door panels are the most visible element of this piece so I spent a bit of time choosing the best grain orientation for these. Although the grain runs in the same direction, these panels were actually cut from different boards that were differently angled. The other thing to remember is that as you plane the wood the grain changes so more adjustments may need to be made. When selecting

wood for the door stiles aim for balance in the grain as well. By moving boards around in different arrangements you will see how the effect can change.

Machining the wood

The cutting list shows the dimensions of the components you will need to machine. The wood was machined with all the parts left longer to allow for trimming later. When you machine plane wood the ends of the boards often suffer a degree of snipe. It is better then to saw around 50mm (2") off the ends of planed boards to get to the good stuff. Always machine up some extra pieces to use as test pieces for setting up things like miter cuts and routing.

Cut and glue the carcase

After setting up for the miter on my tablesaw and checking some test pieces, the sides, top and base were sawn at 45° (**photo 1**). **Photo 2** shows how I used a biscuit joint at the miter but you could also use a domino or dowels. I find biscuit joints fast and accurate. Sand the insides of the boards and glue the top, base and sides together. I used light cramps with wood blocks and the miters closed up fine.

Cut and glue in the shelves

The shelves, which are ³/₁₆" (5mm) less in width than the outer pieces

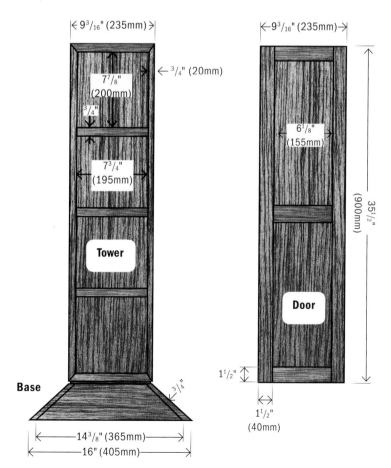

Tower

9³/₁₆" (235mm)
7⁷/₈" (200mm)
³/₄" (20mm)
³/₄
7³/₄" (195mm)

Base
³/₄
14³/₈" (365mm)
16" (405mm)

Door

9³/₁₆" (235mm)
6¹/₈" (155mm)
35¹/₂" (900mm)
1¹/₂"
1¹/₂" (40mm)

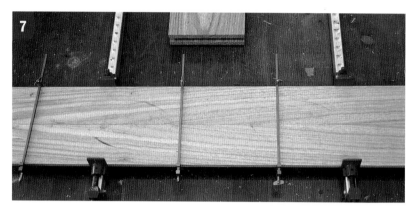

can be sawn to length and sanded. I marked the position of these, applied glue and pushed them in place, then applied the clamps (**photo 3**).

Dowels were used to secure the shelves in place. The dowel heads (these are Miller dowels) add a decorative touch. You can also buy dowels off the shelf from timber yards and hardware stores, or make your own with a dowel plate. The dowel positions are marked (**photo 4**), holes drilled (**photo 5**) and dowels glued in (**photo 6**).

Door and back panel

The door and back frames are made at the same time as they are identical in construction. For the door panel I had two short pieces of white cedar that were wide enough but the grain did not quite match. It would have been better of course to have one long piece to cut the two door panels from. What I did was juggle the grain around to get the appearance of one matched board. Did I succeed? In **photo 7** I am gluing the back panel together from two narrow pieces.

Jointing the door

The joint used for the door can be a mortise and tenon, a floating tenon, domino or dowels. I used the router to make the mortises and made up loose tenons from white cedar (**photo 8**). **Photo 9** shows a sample of an alternative joint with two dowels.

The door frame encloses a solid timber panel, $^3/_8$" (10mm) thick.

CUTTING LIST

Measurements in inches/mm

QTY	COMPONENT	LENGTH	WIDTH	THICKNESS
	Carcase			
2	sides	35$^1/_2$ (900)	5$^3/_4$ (145)	$^3/_4$ (20)
2	carcase top/base	9$^1/_4$ (235)	5$^3/_4$ (145)	$^3/_4$ (20)
3	shelves	7$^3/_4$ (195)	5$^1/_2$ (140)	$^3/_4$ (20)
	Door and back panel			
4	door/back panel stiles	35$^1/_2$ (900)	1$^1/_2$ (40)	$^3/_4$ (20)
6	door/back panel rails	6$^1/_8$ (155)	1$^1/_2$ (40)	$^3/_4$ (20)
2	panels (cut to fit)	32$^1/_4$ (820)	6$^7/_8$ (175)	$^3/_8$ (10)
	Base			
	sides	6$^1/_4$ (160)	7$^1/_4$ (185)	$^3/_4$ (20)
	front/back	14$^3/_8$ (365)	3$^3/_4$ (95)	$^3/_4$ (20)
	panel	8$^3/_4$ (220)	6$^1/_2$ (165)	$^3/_8$ (10)

The panel is housed in a groove. Before cutting the groove on a router table I removed part of the waste by making a saw cut on the tablesaw (**photo 10**). This makes the work of the router a little easier.

Spend some time aligning the fence and router cutter perfectly (**photo 11**). Theoretically you can run the wood over the router cutter and then flip it and run the other face against the fence of the router table. However, I have tried this and found that every now and then one piece of wood can be grabbed by the cutter and flung across the workshop. Hence, I prefer only making one pass over the router table.

Glue up the door and back

Photo 12 shows mortised and grooved components. All the wood machining should now have been completed. In **photo 13** the back is shown layed out and ready to be assembled. Sand the panels before assembly.

If you wish, do a test assembly of the door and back without glue; once you are happy with everything apply glue and clamp up (**photo 14**). Leave overnight if possible.

Make the base

The photo at the start of this story shows how the base is constructed with the sides mitered across the grain and the front and back mitered on the face. A biscuit join connects the pieces. I spent time getting the top edges flush to keep the unit without twist and to avoid having to spend time planing the edges flush later (**photo 15**). An offcut from the door panels was glued in place on top of the base.

Fitting the door

I used butt hinges and these were carefully recessed into position (**photos 16, 17**). You can use a laminate trimmer or small router to cut out the recess for the hinge. I have started using a router hand plane for this sort of work and find this far superior for small jobs like this. The router plane is quiet, fast to set up and without the racket and danger of an electric router.

I decided to opt for a routed fingerpull near the top of the door instead of a knob. Instead of a catch I fitted rare earth magnets into some countersunk holes just above the fingerpull (**photo 18**).

Assembly and polishing

The tower is fixed to the base by screwing in four screws from underneath. A small panel separates the cabinet from the base (**photo 19**). I fixed the back panel to the tower with screws in countersunk holes. Wood plugs go in the holes to hide the screws. You could just glue on the back but it is easier to polish the piece without the back on, better to polish everything first, fix the back then tap in the wood plugs and touch up the plugs with polish. **Photo 20** shows the cabinet prior to polishing with shellac and wax.

18
The finger groove and magnets.

19
Shows the small panel which separates the base from the tower.

Old Douglas fir and
precious Huon pine
complement each other
in this storage cabinet.

Collector's Cabinet

Sawing grooves in the frame components on the panel saw. Always use pushsticks when working at the tablesaw.

The stopped grooves on the legs were cut with the router.

Assembly in progress.

Components for one of the sides prepared for assembly. A test dry fit will ensure everything goes together correctly.

This particular cabinet was made to house a client's large CD collection, however it can be used for any storage needs. The theme of the design is the square, as evidenced by the square main frame components and the top. The sides and door are a frame and panel construction. I made the door panels by gluing two thicknesses of Huon pine veneer together. To keep the weight of the cabinet down the shelves were made from $1/4$" (6mm) plywood edged with a solid timber strip.

A beam reclaimed from a building site provided me with a small amount of recycled Douglas fir. With careful resawing there was enough wood for the cabinet frame components. The panels are made from Huon pine. Both these timbers are slow growing conifers and have similar and complementary color shades.

The legs and the upper and lower rails are $1^5/_8$"x $1^5/_8$" (42 x 42mm) while the middle rails are 1"x1" (25 x 25mm). The legs were cut to length $47^1/_4$" (1200mm) and all the rails were then cut to $11^3/_4$" (300mm). At the back there are three evenly spaced 2" x $3/_4$" (50 x 20mm) rails that the plywood back is fixed to.

Dowel joinery

The rails and legs are joined with dowels. Care is needed in laying out the position of the dowels because they need to clear each other in the leg at the corners and also clear the grooves for the panels. I used two dowels in each rail—in **photos 3 and 5** you can see how these are placed. The top and lower rails use $7/_{16}$" (11mm) dowels whie the smaller center rails use $3/_8$" (9.5mm) dowels. The side rails are evenly spaced along the leg.

With the dowel holes all drilled the next step is to cut the grooves for the solid panels on the sides. The grooves in this case are $1/_4$" (5mm) wide although they can be whatever size you like. The rails can all have their grooves cut on the tablesaw as in **photo 1**. The grooves on the legs though are stopped and so these were cut with the router. With a fence attached the grooves are cut with a straight cutter. The groove in this case runs in-between the dowel holes on the leg (**photo 2**).

There are also grooves required to house the top panel. These are run in the top rails on the tablesaw. Some further work is required later to extend the groove into the leg corner to accept the top panel.

Preparing the panels

The solid timber panels were then prepared. These are $1/4$" (5mm) thick and should be a neat but definitely not tight fit in the grooves. Once all the drilling and routing is complete a test assembly can be done with the components. **Photo 3** shows how the sides go together. When you are happy with the fit of the components glue both sides together, checking everything is flat and square. **Photo 4** shows how the side panels drop into place.

Before the rest of the unit can be glued up the top panel must be prepared and cut to size. In this case I book-matched two pieces of Huon and then routed a shallow groove in the middle of the panel and glued in a strip of Douglas fir.

When this was dry I planed the Douglas fir strip flush and then routed another shallow groove in at right angles and again glued in a Douglas fir strip which was also flushed off when dry. The grooves in the top rails need to be extended into the corners of the legs to accept the top panel. I used a router and chisel to achieve this. **Photo 7** shows how the top panel looks when complete.

When everything is ready the rest of the cabinet can be glued up, including the front and rear rails and the top panel.

Door

With the cabinet glue-up complete the door can be made. The door rails and stiles use $1^1/8$"x $3/4$" (30 x 20mm) timber with the four center rails made to 1"x $3/4$" (25 x 20mm). The door joints use small floating tenons at the corners and dowels for the center rails as shown in **photo 5**. The door frame is a little smaller than the opening and the

center door rails importantly must be positioned to match the side rails. Lay out the rail positions on the stiles and check they are going to line up with the rails on the cabinet sides. Before gluing up the door I ran the center rails over the planer and took off $1/16$" (2mm); this sets the rails in a little rather than being flush with the front of the stiles. I think it looks better like this.

While the door frame is drying the panels for the doors can be made up. I used some figured Huon pine veneer and glued two pieces together making my own 2-ply. **Photo 6** shows the veneer ready to be glued between some MDF cauls. I gave the veneer a sand with coarse paper to key it for gluing.

When the door is dry it can be cleaned up and a rebate run on the inside of the back. This will house the 2-ply panels. The rebate is run with a router bit and the depth is carefully set to equal the thickness of the 2-ply as in **photo 8**. The 2-ply was

5

The door use small floating tenons at the corners and dowels for the center rails.

6

Small sheets of veneer ready to be glued between MDF cauls.

7

The top panel with its inlaid Douglas fir strips.

8

A rebate on the inside of the back of the doors accepts the ply panels.

9

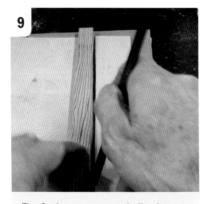

The 2-ply was sawn and sliced to length and width.

10

11

The corners were rounded with a chisel to fit the curve of the rebate.

12

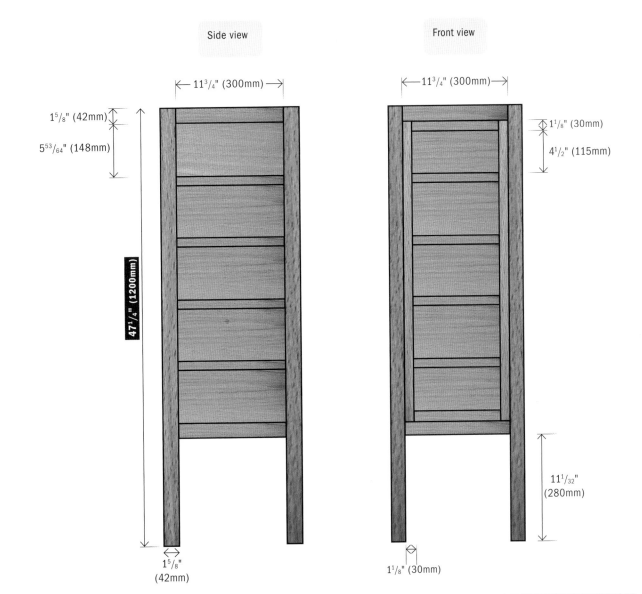

Side view

Front view

11³/₄" (300mm)

11³/₄" (300mm)

1⁵/₈" (42mm)

5⁵³/₆₄" (148mm)

47¹/₄" (1200mm)

1¹/₈" (30mm)

4¹/₂" (115mm)

11¹/₃₂"
(280mm)

1⁵/₈"
(42mm)

1¹/₈" (30mm)

cut and sawn to length and width as in **photos 9 and 10**. The corners were rounded with a chisel (**photo 11**) to fit the curve of the rebate as in **photo 12**. The 2-ply needs to be a very precise fit so spend some time here adjusting and gently planing as needed. The panels can be glued in place when ready; they should be flush with the door frame when complete, requiring a light sand only. Be careful because the 2-ply is not that strong. If you are concerned about this weak point then you can use three veneer layers and make your own 3-ply, which will be stronger.

The door is fitted with brass butt hinges to the cabinet. In this case

CUTTING LIST

Measurements in inches/mm
*approx

QTY	COMPONENT	LENGTH	WIDTH	THICKNESS
4	legs	47¹/₄ (1200)	1⁵/₈ (42)	1⁵/₈ (42)
8	rails	11³/₄ (300)	1⁵/₈ (42)	1⁵/₈ (42)
8	center rails	11³/₄ (300)	1 (25)	1 (25)
3	rear rails	11³/₄ (300)	2 (50)	³/₄ (20)
10	side panels	12¹/₂ (320)	6³/₄ (170)	³/₁₆ (5)*
	top panel	12¹/₂ (320)	12¹/₂ (320)	³/₁₆ (5)
2	door	32⁷/₈ (835)	1¹/₈ (30)	³/₄ (20)*
2		9³/₈ (238)	1¹/₈ (30)	³/₄ (20)*
4		9³/₈ (238)	1 (25)	³/₄ (20)
5	door panels	10 (255)	6¹/₂ (165)	¹/₁₆ (1.2)
5	shelves	13³/₈ (340)	11³/₄ (300)	¹/₄ (6)*

The shelves sit on the side center rails.

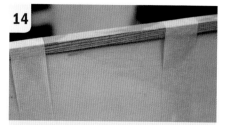

The shelves are edged with oregon strips taped in place and planed flush when dry.

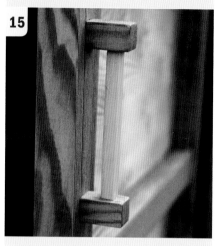

The handle was made from oregon end pieces with a Huon pine pull.

I set the door frame into the cabinet about ¹/₄" (6mm) rather than setting it flush with the outside of the legs because I thought it looked more interesting. You can see this on the main photo.

The shelves now need to be made. I used some 6mm thick hoop pine ply. The shelves sit on the side center rails (**photo 13**) while the bottom shelf required small cleats to be fixed on the lower rails to support it. The shelves are edged with thin Douglas fir strips glued on with masking tape to hold them till the glue dried (**photo 14**). The edges were planed flush when dry.

Handmade handle

The door handle was made with two small ⁷/₁₆ x ⁷/₁₆" (11 x 11mm) Douglas fir sections holding a ¹/₄ x ¹/₄" (6 x 6mm) Huon pine grab. The Douglas fir is screwed to the door stile and the Huon grab is rounded at the ends to fit into small holes in the Douglas fir (**photo 15**). I found the door handle very fiddly to make and the first one I made split.

To secure the door 6mm (¹/₄") diameter magnets are glued into holes at the top and bottom of the door. The pull of the magnets is just right as the door closes with a satisfying click. The back was fitted last. Small cleats were tacked onto the rear frame and the ply back was then screwed into position.

Oil finish

Choosing a finish is always personal. I chose to use a furniture oil because I like the matt look and smooth feel which this can give. The whole cabinet was given its final sand and four coats of oil were applied with a soft cloth. Each coat was allowed to thoroughly dry before the next was applied. After the first coat was dry I gave the cabinet a light scuff with fine sandpaper before applying the next coat. The final coat was buffed to a soft glow.

A finish like this is suitable for a non-working surface but there is no reason why a sprayed finish could not be used. Personal preference will guide you.

I found this cabinet an enjoyable project to make. The scale is fairly small but very approachable with regard to cutting all the joints. Depending on the collection you need to house, the spacing of the shelves can also be easily modified. If the idea of gluing up your own ply panels doesn't appeal to you it would be a simple matter to redesign the cabinet with solid panels in the door.

'China' Cabinet

Inspired by Chinese
period furniture, this
cabinet is somewhat
challenging to build.

The inspiration for this piece came from Gustav Ecke's book *Chinese Domestic Furniture*. I figured out how to make it from a picture in the book. There were scale drawings which helped, although I changed all the measurements. The legs all angle out and are joined front, back and sides by square rails. Between the rails on the sides and back are panels. The top sits on the ends of the legs. The main features are the splayed legs, beading on the rails and the curve of the top ends.

I don't like machining—it's noisy, dusty and dangerous—so I try and get some common sizes happening to streamline things. For this reason the legs and rails are both 1⁵/₈" (42mm) thick. The frame for the top is also 1⁵/₈" thick. I would have preferred a thickness of 1³/₄" (45mm) but I couldn't get this out of the flitch I used. The latter was slab of blackwood 8" (200mm) thick and 12" (300mm) wide which despite some large cracks and holes, had beautiful color and grain. I sawed out the legs, rails and side panels but couldn't get enough quality wood for the drawer fronts or top. I bought extra wood for these parts but had a hard time finding wood that had a satisfying grain pattern.

Construction

The 2³/₄" (70mm) wide legs are flush with the rails, as they are both 1⁵/₈" thick. Keeping them flush also makes it easier to make the mortise and tenons. These can be machined with the same tooling settings on your mortiser or jointing tool.

I had some concern about using a 1⁵/₈" square length of wood over a distance of 39³/₄" (1000mm) for the horizontal rails. However the upper rail is strutted with the drawer divider and two drawer runners in the middle, and the lower rail does have a center rail strutting it to the back.

The angle of the leg is 3° (or 87° depending how you want to read it). The legs were sawn at this angle as were the front and back rails. I used the drop saw for this. Care is needed to correctly saw the angles on the rails at both ends. I cut the

All the frame joints are loose tenons. A double tenon is used for each joint.

I made up a small test piece to check the way the bead would be run. I first used a cutter, then a handmade scraper.

The bead was run and components sanded prior to gluing up.

Glue is applied to the joints and then the parts brought together.

legs and placed them on the bench, then positioned the rails to get the actual length, noting that the lower rails are longer than the upper rails. The side rails, drawer runners and lower middle rail are all the same length. The two center drawer runners are made from $1^5/_8$" (42mm) square blackwood. The vertical drawer divider was sawn to $5^1/_4$" (135mm) with the flap opening also set at $5^1/_4$".

The joints

The main joint through the whole cabinet is a floating tenon, in this case dominos were used (**photo 1**). Without a joint cutter like this the other options are to use a mortising table and slot cutter or with appropriate jigs a plunge router. Naturally you could cut mortise and tenons in the traditional way or use large dowels.

The 3° angle on the legs and the ends of the rails poses a problem in getting the mortise to enter at 90°. The edge of the wood cannot be used to register from whatever way the mortise is cut. To solve this I made some 3° wedges and taped these on the edge where the joint was to be cut. The domino tool (or mortise table) then sat on the wedge, meaning the cutter entered the wood at 3° to its face. The legs and the side rails are jointed easily because they meet at 90°.

Bead

A bead runs around the face edge of the front and also on the side rails. After testing on a scrap (**photo 2** I used a laminate trimmer with a beading cutter to run the mould along all the rails. A flat (unrouted area) was left on the top where the rail meets the vertical divider. The legs were also moulded but again a flat was left where the rails meet. The bead has to be hand cut at the intersections and this is done much later after the whole carcase is assembled.

Panels

The back and sides have floating panels which sit in grooves between the legs and rails. The panel thickness is $3/_8$" (10mm) with the side panels blackwood and the rear ones of Huon pine. I often use blackwood and Huon together, the contrast is excellent. The back panels need to be sawn at the 3° like the frames. The rail grooves were cut on the tablesaw. The saw kerf is about $1/_8$" (3.5mm) wide so this meant passing the rails over the saw four times. The wood is passed over the saw then flipped and run through again making the groove self centring. Grooves also have to be made in the legs but these can't be cut on the tablesaw because they are stopped grooves, hence the plunge router is the tool of choice for this operation (**photo 6**).

Gluing up front and back

With all the components machined and jointed now is the time to sand parts that will be difficult to access once assembled. Some places though are better not to sand (for instance the inside edges of the legs) because the rails connect here and it is better to have a clean flat edge. A hand plane can be run along these edges (**photo 3**).

The front and back frames can now be glued up (**photo 4, 5**). The front is straightforward but make sure the joint in the middle of the top rail for the vertical drawer divider is cut first. The back needs the panels fitted in to the grooves at glue-up (**photo 6**). Both back panels should be placed in their grooves at glue-up because the ends of these are at 3° (the upper side panels can be put aside as these can be slid in place

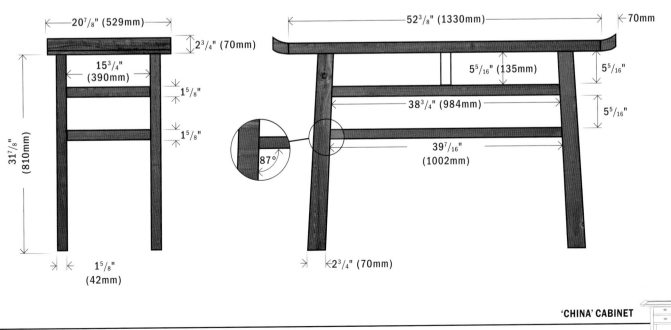

later). I forgot to put in the upper back panel and had to manoeuvre it in later. Always check the frames are gluing up flat without twist. Because there are no 90° angles on these frames set a bevel gauge and use this to check all the angles are the same in the corners. If the angle is too great, angle the clamp away from the corner doing the opposite if the angle is too small. With the glue dry the rails and legs can be planed and sanded flush where needed (**photo 7**).

Bead extension

The bead can now be carved and extended into the corners. To do this I used a straight chisel and made a scraper to cut the flat groove. The scraper was made from a hacksaw blade ground to shape with a sharpened edge. The outside edge of the legs is rounded over and this is done now. I ran a router over the edge to remove some of the waste (**photo 8**) and also give me a clear line to follow later with a handplane (**photo 9**).

Gluing up the frame assembly

Ensure that the side panels fit neatly in their grooves and that you select the best face to be on the outside. With everything sanded and checked the carcase can now be glued up.

Lay the back down and glue in all rails and slide in the lower side panels (**photo 10**). The panels are not glued and should be able to move a little in width to allow for wood movement (**photo 11**). With glue applied bring the front frame to the rails and tap it in place. Moving quickly, apply clamps and check everything for square. I sight along the sides and fronts to see they are parallel, if not adjust as needed. What is missing now is the vertical drawer divider, the top, the drawer guides and the internal shelf (**photo 12**).

Shelf

The shelf is two $^1/_2$" (12mm) thick Huon pine boards shiplapped in the middle with two cleats supporting the shelf at the ends. The cleats are $^1/_2$" square blackwood glued and

fixed to the lower side rails. The shelf is supported in the center with the lower middle rail. Another cleat is glued in place on top of the shelf boards to permanently secure them. The cleats are glued to the rails—glue is only applied to half of the width of the shelf to allow for wood movement. To prevent the shelf rattling a dowel was fixed through the shelf into the rail underneath.

Drawer guides

The middle drawer guide is $1^5/_8$" (42mm) wide (the same as the vertical divider) and sits on the middle runners. Two side drawer runners are fixed to the sides of the middle rails and on top of these were fixed the outer drawer guides. The runners and guides were glued and secured with dowels. You could use screws instead of the dowels but I was trying to keep metal use to a minimum—at the moment the plan is to have no metal except for the flap hinges.

The top

This is a frame and panel construction. The long rails of the frame are $2^3/_4$" wide (70mm) and $1^5/_8$" (42mm) thick with the end rails $2^3/_4$" (70mm) square. The panel is $^3/_4$" (20mm) thick. Choose the grain carefully for the top and note the end grain on the end rails. I have the grain pattern following the curve. The panel has a rebate on the edges with the tongue fitting in a matching groove in the frame. The groove runs the length of the long rails but is a stopped

5

Front legs and rails in clamps. Note the bead doesn't reach the corners.

7

The back asssembly ready to be glued together. The panel is Huon pine.

6

The back and front assemblies after glue up. Note the grooves in the legs to accept the side panels.

8

Legs are profiled on the outer edge. A router cutter removed the waste.

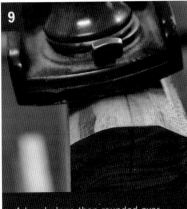

9

A hand plane then rounded over the profile to final size.

10

Beginning the glue-up—the center rails are in place.

Side panels and rails being positioned in glue-up.

groove on the end rails. Long floating tenons join the rails to the ends (**photo 13, 14**).

With the joints cut, remove as much wood as possible from the end rails to follow the concave curve. I rip-sawed a number of cuts to remove waste (**photo 15**). Then it was time for saw, chisel and hammer to remove the bulk of the wood. An old moulding plane that I bought 20 years ago was used for the first time to work the curve, after that it was carving with a gouge and then sanding (**photo 16**). You'll also need to make the groove in the underneath of the top for the upper edge of the back panel. This can be made with a router. Before any gluing run the bead along the front edge with a laminate trimmer—it's easier to do at this stage. The convex edge was left till later and the square edge supports the clamps when the frame and panel is glued up. After the glue is dry

the convex curve can be worked. An electric plane hogged off most of the waste and then a handplane cleaned up the final shape.

The joint where the short vertical drawer divider meets the top can now be made. I used $1/2$" (12mm) dowels to join the top to the legs. Marks for the dowel holes were made and holes drilled in the tops of the legs with matching holes in the underneath of the top.

At this stage check for anything else that needs doing prior to the final glue-up. There are no top drawer kickers yet, important components that prevent the drawer tipping down when it is pulled out. I decided to inset two pieces of $1^5/8$ x $1/2$" (42mm x 12mm) blackwood underneath the top to act as kickers. These are dovetailed into the frame. Notches were made underneath the top to house the corners of the side panels.

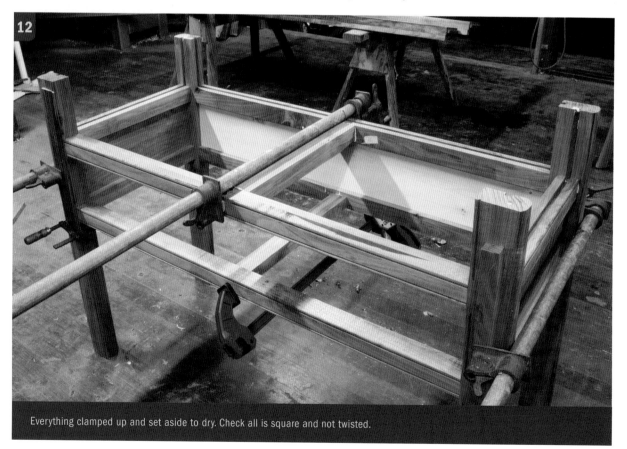

Everything clamped up and set aside to dry. Check all is square and not twisted.

With everything checked for fit and any sanding completed the top can be glued to the carcase. This also entails fitting at the same time the upper side panels and vertical drawer divider.

Drawers and flap

The drawer fronts are blackwood with Huon pine sides and backs. A blackwood veneered plywood panel completes the drawer. The flap is a solid piece of blackwood. Selecting the grain pattern for the flap and drawers was a real killer. At one point I had machined two matching pieces of wood with beautiful grain but rejected them because the grain pattern sloped and made the cabinet appear to lean to the side. I eventually settled for some rather plain wood but with a curve in the pattern that gives the cabinet an uplifting look.

The drawer fronts have one edge that is sawn at 3° and the other at 90°. The drawer sides are different widths—the angled side was made slightly wider with the projecting width planed flush after the drawers were glued up. The flap has the same 3° angle on both ends and is mounted with brass hinges in the usual manner.

Bead and handles

The bead along the top has to be extended along the curved ends. To do this I made up a scratchstock. A bandsaw kerf holds a piece of hacksaw blade and three screws lock the blade. Slowly form the groove by running the scratchstock along the wood. This was a little tricky and it pays to make a practice bead on an offcut before working the real edge. A chisel and sandpaper complete the bead.

The drawers and flap need handles of some sort and here the options are pretty open. I agonised over it and drilled a 1³/₄" (45mm) hole

around ³/₈" (10mm) deep using a forstner bit. Then small pieces of wood were cut and shaped. These are secured with screws from the inside. Just gluing the handles on will not last.

Drawer stops of small pieces of wood were glued at the back of the drawer runners. The drawers stop just back from the edge of the bead. Magnets act as catches for the flap.

Polishing

The whole cabinet needs to be completely checked and hand sanded. Any bruises can be ironed out and any holes can be filled with matching putty (always go darker than lighter with putty color). Gold leaf was applied to the handle recesses as a contrast. The piece was given three coats of shellac followed by wax which was hand rubbed to a smooth lustre.

13

The mortises in the end rails of the top. The wood was very hard and hence I drilled out most of the waste (lower piece) before using the mortiser (upper piece).

14

The floating tenon shown where it meets the mortise in the end rail.

15

A series of saw cuts removed much of the waste on the ends. Note the end grain pattern follows the curve.

16

A chisel and old round bottom moulding plane were used to complete the curve.

Useful metric/imperial conversions rounded to the nearest millimeter.

Inches	MM
0.039	1
¹⁄₁₆	2
⅛	3
¼	6
⅜	10
½	12
⁹⁄₁₆	14
¾	20
⅞	22
1	25

Divide mm by 25 to get inches

50mm divided by 25 equals 2 inches
10mm divided by 25 equals .40 inches

Multiply inches by 25 to get mm

2 inches x 25 equals 50mm
½ inch x 25 equals (.50 x 25) = 12.5 mm

1 millimeter equals .03937 inch
1 inch equals 25.40 mm